Current
CONTROVERSIES

Guns and Violence

DATE DUE

Other Books in the Current Controversies Series

Guns and Violence

Debra A. Miller, Book Editor

GREENHAVEN PRESS
A part of Gale, Cengage Learning

Detroit • New York • San Francisco • New Haven, Conn • Waterville, Maine • London

Christine Nasso, *Publisher*
Elizabeth Des Chenes, *Managing Editor*

© 2009 Greenhaven Press, a part of Gale, Cengage Learning

For more information, contact:
Greenhaven Press
27500 Drake Rd.
Farmington Hills, MI 48331-3535
Or you can visit our Internet site at gale.cengage.com

For product information and technology assistance, contact us at

Gale Customer Support, 1-800-877-4253
For permission to use material from this text or product, submit all requests online at www.cengage.com/permissions

Further permissions questions can be emailed to permissionrequest@cengage.com

Articles in Greenhaven Press anthologies are often edited for length to meet page requirements. In addition, original titles of these works are changed to clearly present the main thesis and to explicitly indicate the author's opinion. Every effort is made to ensure that Greenhaven Press accurately reflects the original intent of the authors. Every effort has been made to trace the owners of copyrighted material.

Cover image copyright Sascha Burkard, 2008. Used under license from Shutterstock.com.

LIBRARY OF CONGRESS CATALOGING-IN-PUBLICATION DATA

Guns and violence / Debra A. Miller, book editor.
    p. cm. -- (Current controversies)
    Includes bibliographical references and index.
    ISBN 978-0-7377-4320-3 (hardcover)
    ISBN 978-0-7377-4319-7 (pbk.)
    1. Gun control--United States. 2. Violence--United States. 3. Firearms--Law and legislation--United States. 4. Firearms ownership--United States. I. Miller, Debra A.
    HV7436.G87746 2009
    363.330973--dc22
                                                                2008045075

Printed in the United States of America
1 2 3 4 5 6 7 13 12 11 10 09

Contents

Chapter 1: Is Gun Violence a Serious Problem?

Yes: Gun Violence Is a Serious Problem

No: Gun Violence Is Not a Serious Problem

Chapter 2: Can Gun Control Measures Reduce Gun Violence?

Yes: Gun Control Measures Can Reduce Gun Violence

Chapter 3: Is Gun Control Constitutional?

Yes: Gun Control Is Constitutional

No: Gun Control Is Not Constitutional

Chapter 4: Is Gun Ownership Dangerous?

Foreword

By definition, controversies are "discussions of questions in which opposing opinions clash" (Webster's Twentieth Century Dictionary Unabridged). Few would deny that controversies are a pervasive part of the human condition and exist on virtually every level of human enterprise. Controversies transpire between individuals and among groups, within nations and between nations. Controversies supply the grist necessary for progress by providing challenges and challengers to the status quo. They also create atmospheres where strife and warfare can flourish. A world without controversies would be a peaceful world; but it also would be, by and large, static and prosaic.

The Series' Purpose

The purpose of the *Current Controversies* series is to explore many of the social, political, and economic controversies dominating the national and international scenes today. Titles selected for inclusion in the series are highly focused and specific. For example, from the larger category of criminal justice, *Current Controversies* deals with specific topics such as police brutality, gun control, white collar crime, and others. The debates in *Current Controversies* also are presented in a useful, timeless fashion. Articles and book excerpts included in each title are selected if they contribute valuable, long-range ideas to the overall debate. And wherever possible, current information is enhanced with historical documents and other relevant materials. Thus, while individual titles are current in focus, every effort is made to ensure that they will not become quickly outdated. Books in the *Current Controversies* series will remain important resources for librarians, teachers, and students for many years.

In addition to keeping the titles focused and specific, great care is taken in the editorial format of each book in the series. Book introductions and chapter prefaces are offered to provide background material for readers. Chapters are organized around several key questions that are answered with diverse opinions representing all points on the political spectrum. Materials in each chapter include opinions in which authors clearly disagree as well as alternative opinions in which authors may agree on a broader issue but disagree on the possible solutions. In this way, the content of each volume in *Current Controversies* mirrors the mosaic of opinions encountered in society. Readers will quickly realize that there are many viable answers to these complex issues. By questioning each author's conclusions, students and casual readers can begin to develop the critical thinking skills so important to evaluating opinionated material.

Current Controversies is also ideal for controlled research. Each anthology in the series is composed of primary sources taken from a wide gamut of informational categories including periodicals, newspapers, books, U.S. and foreign government documents, and the publications of private and public organizations. Readers will find factual support for reports, debates, and research papers covering all areas of important issues. In addition, an annotated table of contents, an index, a book and periodical bibliography, and a list of organizations to contact are included in each book to expedite further research.

Perhaps more than ever before in history, people are confronted with diverse and contradictory information. During the Persian Gulf War, for example, the public was not only treated to minute-to-minute coverage of the war, it was also inundated with critiques of the coverage and countless analyses of the factors motivating U.S. involvement. Being able to sort through the plethora of opinions accompanying today's major issues, and to draw one's own conclusions, can be a complicated and frustrating struggle. It is the editors' hope that *Current Controversies* will help readers with this struggle.

Introduction

"Since the early days of the nation's history ... American society has changed dramatically, causing many people to question the value and wisdom of allowing ordinary citizens to own and use guns."

When the United States was founded over 200 years ago, gun ownership was widespread. Most everyone owned guns and used them to protect their homes and families against wild animals and criminal intruders. The nation's founders, who led America's revolution against the British, also considered firearms necessary to protect the nation both against foreign threats and as a check against excessive government power. They envisioned a United States without a standing army, dependent instead on local militias made up of citizen gun owners. These views led to the inclusion of a right to bear arms in the Second Amendment of the Bill of Rights, part of the U.S. Constitution. The amendment, ratified in 1791, provided: "A well-regulated militia being necessary to the security of a free state, the right of the people to keep and bear arms shall not be infringed."

Since the early days of the nation's history, however, American society has changed dramatically, causing many people to question the value and wisdom of allowing ordinary citizens to own and use guns. Various incidents of gun violence through the years have caused the federal government to enact a series of national gun control laws that have placed restrictions on Americans' constitutional gun rights.

Gun Control Laws

The first federal gun control laws were the National Firearms Act of 1934 and the Federal Firearms Act of 1938. These laws were inspired by a culture of lawlessness and gangster violence that developed during Prohibition, a period following World War I when the United States banned the manufacture, sales, import, and export of intoxicating liquors. Despite the ban, there continued to be a huge market for alcohol, and criminal gangs arose in American cities during the 1920s to sell beer and hard liquor to the public. Prohibition was ended in 1933, but the era became known for violent gun battles between gangsters and federal agents trying to enforce the government's alcohol ban, both sides using automatic-fire machine guns on public streets. The legislation of 1934 regulated possession of these and other weapons, imposed a $200 tax on all gun sales, and required gun purchasers to register guns with proper authorities. The 1938 act required sellers of firearms to obtain a federal license and to record the names and addresses of all purchasers. This law also prohibited gun sales to persons without a gun permit and those convicted of certain crimes.

Gun control next became popular in the 1960s, after assassins took the lives of President John F. Kennedy, presidential candidate Robert Kennedy, and civil rights leader Martin Luther King Jr. The result was the Gun Control Act of 1968, which expanded seller license requirements, required more detailed record-keeping, restricted the sale of guns across state lines, and prohibited the sale of guns to felons, the mentally incompetent, drug users, and others. The law also banned mail-order rifles and shotguns, which previously could be ordered by anyone simply by signing a statement indicating they were older than 18 years of age.

Another significant federal gun control law was the Brady Handgun Violence Prevention Act of 1994. This legislation was named for James Brady, a White House press secretary who was shot and severely wounded by John Hinckley, a man with mental problems, during an assassination attempt on President Ronald Reagan in 1981. Following the shooting, Brady's wife Sarah and other supporters founded Handgun

Control Inc., an advocacy group that lobbied for more restrictive gun control laws. The group succeeded in achieving some of its aims with the passage of the 1994 act. It imposed a five-day waiting period and background check before a licensed gun importer, manufacturer, or dealer could sell or deliver a handgun to a buyer. The federal five-day waiting period clause expired in 1998 and was replaced by a mandatory, computerized National Instant Check System (NICS), which provides information for criminal background checks on all firearm purchasers, not just those buying handguns. Many states, however, continue to impose waiting periods in addition to background checks.

The Brady law as passed in 1994 also prohibited teenagers from possessing or selling handguns, barred firearms possession by persons subject to a restraining order because of threats of domestic violence, and banned the manufacture and possession of so-called assault weapons—that is, semiautomatic weapons designed to be fired from the hip with large-capacity ammunition-feeding magazines—for civilian use.

The Brady assault weapons ban, however, expired in 2004 and was not renewed by Congress. Nor has Congress recently passed any other major gun control measures, despite repeated pressure from gun control advocates. Gun control supporters credit the strength of the gun rights lobby, led by the National Rifle Association (NRA), for this congressional inaction. But the federal stalemate on gun legislation has not stopped states and cities from enacting their own gun control laws, many of them much more restrictive than existing federal gun regulations.

District of Columbia v. Heller

One very tough gun law in Washington, D.C., spawned the first gun rights case to be accepted for review by the U.S. Supreme Court in almost seven decades: *District of Columbia v. Heller*. The D.C. law banned all handguns and imposed a requirement that all firearms in the home be kept unloaded and disassembled or bound by a trigger lock. The lower court in *Heller* held that the law was an unconstitutional restriction on the Second Amendment right to bear arms. The U.S. Supreme Court, in a 5-4 ruling issued on June 26, 2008, upheld the lower court and struck down the D.C. ban on handguns. For the first time, the Court decided the central issue of the gun control debate, holding that the Second Amendment right to bear arms is not limited to service in a militia; it also protects an individual's right to own guns for self-protection. In addition, the Court ruled that the D.C. law—both the absolute ban on handguns and the requirements that other firearms be equipped with trigger locks or kept disassembled—violated this individual right to bear arms.

The Supreme Court decision in *Heller* also gave some guidance on the degree to which the right to own a gun can be regulated by gun control legislation. In *Heller*, the Court specifically said that its ruling would *not* affect long-standing gun regulations prohibiting the possession of firearms by felons or the mentally ill, or laws forbidding the carrying of firearms in places such as schools and government buildings. Without providing details, the Court also indicated that other gun restrictions might be constitutional. Many experts believe the decision could threaten other strict gun control laws in cities such as Chicago and San Francisco, but most expect that federal gun restrictions will stand.

The authors of the viewpoints in *Current Controversies: Guns and Violence* address the many issues raised by gun violence in America, including the seriousness of gun violence, whether gun control measures can reduce this violence, whether such gun control measures are constitutional, and whether guns are an effective means of self-defense.

CHAPTER 1

Is Gun Violence a Serious Problem?

Chapter Preface

April 20, 2009, will mark the tenth anniversary of the day in 1999 when two high school seniors, Dylan Klebold and Eric Harris, carried out a massacre of students and teachers at Columbine High School in the small town of Littleton, Colorado. Equipped with an arsenal of guns, knives, and bombs, the young men planned to set off massive propane bombs in the school cafeteria at lunchtime and then shoot at survivors as they came running out of the school. They originally planned to kill hundreds, but because their two main propane bombs did not work, their master plan failed. Instead, the two teenagers simply walked around the school building and randomly shot people, Klebold armed with a 9-mm semi-automatic handgun and a 12-gauge double-barrel sawed-off shotgun, and Harris carrying a 9-mm carbine rifle and a 12-gauge pump sawed-off shotgun. The guns were all purchased at private gun shows. By the end of the day, the pair had killed twelve students and one teacher, and ultimately, they committed suicide by shooting themselves.

No one really knows why the massacre occurred. In many ways the two boys were normal teenagers; they played sports, loved computers, and worried about dates for the prom. But they also were social outcasts who played violent video games and secretly felt a great deal of anger. Harris created a Web site that he filled with dark musings, and just before the shootings, the two had been arrested for breaking into a van. Psychiatrists differ on their assessments of Klebold's and Harris's mental health, with some finding signs of depression and psychopathy and others believing that the teenagers were simply angry and that restrictions on their computer usage following their van-burglary arrest caused them to turn their anger toward homicidal and suicidal thoughts. Some commentators have also suggested that the boys lashed out because they felt bullied or persecuted by fellow students, and others have noted that they had relatively free access to high-powered, dangerous guns. Yet a 2002 government study concluded that while these facts may be risk factors, there is simply no useful profile of exactly what type of student might engage in school gun violence.

Since the Columbine massacre, similar incidents have occurred at a number of other schools throughout the country. The spree of school gun violence has spread fear and anxiety among students and parents across the nation, because it has shown that gun violence can happen not just in inner cities, but anywhere.

However, experts stress that the chance of a student encountering gun violence at school remains very low. According to the government, fewer than one percent of all homicides among school-age children happen on school grounds, and most students will never experience any type of gun incident at school or college. In the 2005–2006 school year, for example, a joint report from the U.S. Department of Education and the Department of Justice found that 14 young people between the ages of 5 and 18 were killed and 3 committed suicide while at school. According to the report, this means that there was only one youth homicide or suicide at school for every 3.2 million students enrolled during the 2005–2006 school year—a very low risk. Moreover, the government claims that school violence is gradually decreasing; 14 homicides in 2006 compare very favorably with 55 school murders in 1992. Violence has decreased most in schools that have taken aggressive actions to prevent bullying, provide closer supervision of students, and reduce violent behaviors.

Many people cite school violence as a reason to establish stricter gun control bans that would make it tougher for kids to get guns. Various proposals have been made, including laws that would require that guns kept in the home be secured safely in locked facilities or with trigger locks, and laws to strengthen existing gun legislation to make it illegal for children to purchase guns from private or unlicensed individuals. Gun rights advocates, however, believe such laws are an unnecessary restriction on the Second Amendment right to bear arms. They point to the low number of students killed by guns at school and argue that most youth homicides occur away from school grounds. In fact, these critics say more kids are smothered, burned, or otherwise murdered by their parents than are killed by guns at school, so it would be an unwise policy to focus on gun control as the solution for youth homicides.

The debate about school gun violence is part of the much broader question of whether gun violence is truly a serious problem in the United States. Some people see gun violence as an epidemic that kills tens of thousands each year, including many children. Others maintain that most of these deaths are caused by violent criminals armed with guns and that crime, not guns, is the core problem. The authors of the viewpoints in this chapter present some of these differing perspectives.

Gun Violence in the United States Is an Epidemic

Bill Durston

Bill Durston is a former expert marksman in the Marines, an emergency physician, and past president of the Sacramento, California, chapter of Physicians for Social Responsibility, a non-profit advocacy organization.

In an article written in 1992, the President of the American College of Emergency Physicians, Dr. Jack Allison, referred to gun violence in the United States as a "shameful epidemic." On April 16, 2007, 32 students and faculty at Virginia Tech [a university in Blacksburg, Virginia] were killed in this ongoing epidemic. Scores more suffered serious non-fatal physical injuries, and untold others suffered psychological trauma, including devastating losses on the part of the friends and family members of those killed.

Dr. Allison used the word "shameful" in referring to the fact that we, as a country, have not taken definitive steps to curb the preventable epidemic of gun violence. It is easy for U.S. citizens and their leaders to condemn the shooters with adjectives such as "heinous" or "deranged." It is not so easy to acknowledge that while there are disturbed people in other democratic, industrialized countries, the epidemic of gun violence is unique to the United States of America.

Gun-Related Deaths and Injuries in the United States

The mass shooting at Virginia Tech was the most deadly in a long series of mass shootings in schools, workplaces, and other public settings in the United States. After each mass

Bill Durston, "The Shameful Epidemic—Gun Violence in the USA," *DurstonforCongress. org*, April 26, 2007. Reproduced by permission.

shooting, U.S. citizens have typically reacted with shock, sorrow, and disbelief, repeatedly asking themselves, "Why?" Citizens of other democratic, industrialized countries also react with shock and sorrow when they learn of mass shootings in the United States, but not with disbelief. For people who live in other civilized countries that don't have repeated mass shootings, the answer to the question, "Why," is obvious. It's the guns. The single factor that most clearly distinguishes the U.S. from other countries that have much lower rates of gun violence is the widespread availability of firearms in the United States.

High profile mass shootings are only the tip of the iceberg of gun-related deaths and injuries in the United States. Every year, approximately 30,000 U.S. civilians are killed by guns. The number of U.S. civilians killed annually by guns is ten times the number of people killed in the September 11 [2001] terrorist attacks. More U.S. civilians are killed by guns every two years than the total number of U.S. soldiers killed in the entire 11 year Vietnam War.

To protect our youth, and ourselves, we should demand rapid enactment of gun control legislation in the United States.

Gunshot wounds are the second leading cause of death for children ages 10–19 in the United States, with only motor vehicle accidents taking a higher toll. A child in the United States is far more likely to catch a bullet than the measles. The homicide rate for U.S. males ages 15–24 is more than ten times higher than in most other developed countries. The much higher rate of gun violence in the United States as compared with other democratic countries corresponds with a much higher rate of firearm ownership in the U.S. and much less stringent gun control laws.

The Lack of Gun Control Legislation

Following the publication of Dr. Allison's 1992 "Shameful Epidemic" article, Congress did take two important steps to address the epidemic of gun violence in the United States.

The federal Brady Act, requiring background checks for most gun purchasers, and the federal Assault Weapons Ban were both enacted in 1994. Over the following decade, there was a 28% decline in the number of gun-related deaths in the United States. In more recent years, though, the federal government's approach to the ongoing epidemic of gun violence has been no less than shameful. In 1997, the Centers for Disease Control and Prevention [CDC] advocated more stringent gun control laws after publishing a study showing that children under the age of 15 in the United States were 12 times more likely to be killed by guns than children in the other leading 25 industrialized countries of the world. Congress reacted by cutting the CDC's funding for research on firearm-related issues and by placing a permanent ban on the use of federal funding for research advocating gun control.

In the ... years since the mass shooting at Columbine High School [1999, in Littleton, Colorado], Congress has enacted no significant new gun control laws. On the contrary, in 2004 Congress and the President let the federal Assault Weapons Ban expire. In 2005, with litigation pending against a gun store that claimed to have "lost" more than 150 military-style rifles, including the one suspected of being sold illegally to the DC [District of Columbia] snipers, Congress passed legislation giving special protection to gun makers and gun dealers from lawsuits.

Myths About Gun Control

Equally shameful are the myths perpetuated by the gun industry and its associated lobby, the National Rifle Association. These myths include:

Myth #1—The United States owes its democratic freedoms to an armed citizenry.

Fact—Most of the guns used in the American Revolution were imported from France at the beginning of the war, and most men who fought in the revolution turned their guns back in after the war was over. We owe our democratic freedoms to the fact that our forefathers retained their principles, not their guns.

Myth #2—The Second Amendment to the United States guarantees an individual "right to bear arms."

Fact—The U. S. Supreme Court has repeatedly ruled that the Second Amendment, which begins with the phrase, "A well regulated militia," confers a collective right of the states to maintain armed militias, such as the current day National Guard, not an individual right of each and every citizen to own guns. The late U.S. Supreme Court Chief Justice Warren Burger, speaking of the gun lobby's misrepresentation of the Second Amendment, stated, "This has been the subject of one of the greatest pieces of fraud on the American public by special interests that I have ever seen in my lifetime."

Myth #3—Honest citizens should own guns for protection.

Fact—Guns in the homes of honest citizens are much more likely to be used to kill themselves and their family members than to protect against an attacker. In one of the best studies on this subject, it was shown that for every one time a gun in the home was used to kill an attacker, there were 43 gun-related deaths of a household member. The United States has been criticized as a country that loves its guns more than its children. There is no doubt that the students and the faculty members killed in the recent Virginia Tech massacre were dearly loved by those who knew them. But will we as a country be moved enough by the Virginia

Tech tragedy to take definitive steps to reduce the chances of other similar tragedies recurring in the near future? It would be shameful if we did not.

To protect our youth, and ourselves, we should demand rapid enactment of gun control legislation in the United States similar to the regulations in other democratic countries that have much lower rates of gun violence but that still allow legitimate hunters and target shooters to practice their sports. This legislation should include licensing and registration of all firearms; renewal and strengthening of the federal assault weapons ban; repeal of special protections for gun makers and gun dealers; and strict regulations on the sale of handguns. If we do not adopt such regulations, when the next mass shooting occurs, there is no point in asking why the tragedy occurred, but only why we allow the shameful epidemic to continue.

The Number of Crimes Committed with Guns Is Increasing in the United States

Walter F. Roche Jr.

Walter F. Roche Jr. is a reporter for the Los Angeles Times.

The rates of homicide and firearm violence jumped in 2005, ending a decade-long decline, according to a new U.S. Justice Department report that reinforces recent warnings by law-enforcement officials.

An Increase in Gun Violence

The National Crime Victimization Survey, released . . . [in September 2006], found that nationwide, homicides increased 4.8 percent, from 16,140 in 2004 to 16,910 [in 2005]. The biggest increases were reported in the Midwest and the South.

In a statement that accompanied the report, Deputy Attorney General Paul McNulty noted that overall crime data for 2005 showed a continuing decline, but he acknowledged an increase last year in crimes committed with firearms. "Whether the increase from 2004 to 2005 marks a change in the trend toward reduced firearms victimization rates cannot be determined from one year's data," he said. He noted that the 2005 rate was still lower than the rate reported in 2001.

[In 2005] Seattle police investigated 25 homicides, a department spokeswoman said. In 2004, Seattle police investigated 24 slayings, the city's lowest homicide rate in 40 years. A decade earlier, in 1994, police investigated 69 homicides, one of the highest rates in recent years. "We recognize that some jurisdictions are experiencing a recent increase in certain types of violent crime," McNulty said.

Chuck Wexler, executive director of the Police Executive Research Forum, a law-enforcement policy center based in Washington, D.C., said police chiefs from around the country who attended an August forum sponsored by his group reported that the increase in violent crimes first seen in 2005 had continued into this year, particularly in three categories: homicides, robberies and aggravated assaults.

Males, blacks and those under 24 were violent-crime victims more frequently than other groups, such as females, whites and those 25 or older.

The victimization survey follows an FBI [Federal Bureau of Investigation, the nation's top law enforcement agency] report issued in June showing that violent crime increased 2.5 percent in 2005. Wexler said the FBI data, which also showed a substantial rise in the number of homicides, reflected conditions currently experienced by law-enforcement officials. He said that in Sacramento, Calif., for instance, the homicide rate this year [2006] had jumped 45 percent.

The Data

According to the report released Sunday [September 10, 2006], the 2005 overall homicide rate was 5.7 per 100,000 individuals. The homicide rate in the Midwest jumped 5.8 percent from 2004, and it increased 5.3 percent in the South.

Males, blacks and those under 24 were violent-crime victims more frequently than other groups, such as females, whites and those 25 or older.

According to the report, 24 percent of the violent crimes were committed by an armed offender, and the rate of firearm violence jumped from 1.4 individuals per 100,000 in 2004 to 2.0 per 100,000 in 2005.

Overall in 2005, according to the report, U.S. residents age 12 or older were the victims of 18 million property crimes and 5.2 million violent crimes.

An estimated 53 percent of violent crimes and 60 percent of property crimes are never reported to the police.

"This report tells us . . . the serious events—robbery and gun crimes—increased and the FBI already told us homicides increased," said criminal justice professor James Alan Fox of Northeastern University. "So while the report shows the more numerous but least serious violence—simple assaults, which is pushing and shoving—went down, the mix got worse in terms of severity. That wasn't a very good trade-off," Fox said.

The Government's Response

With congressional-elections approaching, these reports could pose political problems for the [George W. Bush] administration, and department officials have been scurrying to understand and deal with the problem.

Unlike the FBI report culled from police blotters, the statistic bureau makes estimates based on interviews with 134,000 people, so it counts not only reported crime but also crimes the police never hear about. Also, an estimated 53 percent of violent crimes and 60 percent of property crimes are never reported to the police.

Statistician Shannan Catalano, who wrote the new report, said the increases in gun violence and robbery rates reinforce the FBI data and the anecdotal evidence from local officials. But she cautioned that so few people in the survey reported robberies that the bureau cannot be certain whether those figures represent a true increase or a random sampling variation.

Because it is based on interviews with people about their firsthand experiences with crimes, the bureau's survey does not include homicides. It also tallies crimes such as simple assault and personal theft that are not covered by the FBI reports.

Professor Alfred Blumstein of Carnegie Mellon University said the rise in gun violence was particularly troubling. "A major police effort to confiscate guns helped bring down the surge in violent crime that occurred in the late 1980s and early 1990s," Blumstein said. "But gun distribution is easier now because we have begun to back off gun control."

Backed by the National Rifle Association [a gun rights advocacy group], the Bush administration has been cool toward gun-control measures.

McNulty noted the record-low rates but said "we are concerned about" an increase in the violent firearm crime rate.

Gun Violence Disproportionately Affects African Americans and Other Minorities

We Need to Stop

We Need to Stop is a Web site featuring blogs about African-American culture.

I was listening to a local talk show [in April 2008] and there was a man on by the name of John Rosenthal from an organization called *Stop Handgun Violence*, and I don't remember the exact figure, but he mentioned the fact that at least 85% of the people killed by handguns are African American. Absolutely stunning. So if you are black, watch your back. He talked about the gun industry, particular guns, how guns are marketed, and the government's sort of chummy relationship with the gun industry. . . .

Fashion Guns

[Some guns] almost look like fashion accessories, ones you'd pick out to match your outfit or you can have a different color for the day of the week. How fashionable. If you are going to kill, why not do it in style? Just what our impressionable young people need—matching guns and outfits.

According to Serf City, the seller and marketer of this line [of fashion guns], is honoring our hoplophobic mayor with a line of brightly colored paints for each of the 5 boroughs—Manhattan red, Bronx rose, Brooklyn blue, Queens green, and Staten Island orange. They even include a stencil of Mayor Mike's [Michael Bloomberg, mayor of New York City] face for the barrel of the gun.

We Need to Stop, "Gun Violence in the African American Community," *www.weneed tostop.com*, April 7, 2008. Reproduced by permission.

Guns in the Wrong Hands

According to The Coalition To Stop Gun Violence, assault rifles can be purchased at gun tradeshows without background checks. One more interesting point made during the interview was the fact that there used to be more gas stations than gun dealers. Now this fact is only true for five states: Alaska, Idaho, Montana, Oregon, and Wyoming. Highly black populated states?

Yes, crime occurs everywhere. But much of the black on black gun violent crime is occurring in [poor black neighborhoods].

We have the right to bear arms, but arms continue to get into the wrong hands. What is the problem with this picture and how can we fix it? I know—guns don't kill. People kill.

Black on Black Gun Crime

If you ever take the time to watch the A & E weekly crime documentary *First 48*, and you will notice a predominant number of black murder gunshot victims cases, with some hispanics too, and most of the alleged perpetrators are black males, in poor black neighborhoods. Yes, crime occurs everywhere. But much of the black on black gun violent crime is occurring in these places. I don't know what kind of contracts these jurisdictions enter into with the cable show for actual filming.

Some people don't like negative statistics, and some quickly dismiss them as conspiracies, inaccuracies, etc., but until I see evidence to counter them, I will have to take what I see as fact. . . .

More Statistics

Gun violence is a priority issue for African Americans and other minorities. Over 368,000 Americans were victims to murders, robberies, and aggravated assaults in 2005 committed by perpetrators carrying a firearm, and the African-American community is one of the hardest hit:

- In 2004, firearm homicide was the number one cause of death for 15–34 year old African Americans.

- In 2004, the firearm death rate for African Americans was twice that of whites.

- In 2004, an African-American male under age 30 was 7.5 times more likely to be murdered than a white male under age 30.

- In 2005, nearly 91 percent of African-American murder victims were slain by African-American offenders.

- In 2004, African-American males accounted for 47 percent of all firearm homicide victims, while they only account for 6 percent of the entire population.

- Firearms have become the predominant method of suicide for African Americans aged 15–24 years, accounting for 56 percent of suicides in 2004.

- In Florida, African-American males have an almost eight times greater chance of dying in a firearm-related homicide than white males. In addition, the firearm-related homicide death rate for African-American females is greater than white males and over four times greater than white females.

America's Gun Culture Is Fading

Gun Guys

GunGuys.com *is a project of the Freedom States Alliance, an organization working to reduce gun violence in America.*

A story from *Reuters* [news service] from Jan. 9th [2008] asked: "Is America, land of shooting massacres in schools and public places, slowly falling out of love with guns?" The answer is yes, and it runs counter to popular perceptions of the United States as a country where most citizens are armed to the teeth and believe it is every American's inalienable right to buy an AK 47-style assault rifle with the minimum of bureaucratic paperwork.

But in fact, gun ownership in the United States has been declining steadily over more than three decades, relegating gun owners to minority status. At the same time, support for stricter gun controls has been growing steadily and those in favor make up a majority.

The Power of the Gun Lobby

This is a little-reported phenomenon but the trend is shown clearly by statistics compiled by the University of Chicago's National Opinion Research Center (NORC), which has been tracking gun ownership and attitudes on firearms since 1972, the longest-running survey on the subject in the United States.

The number of households with guns dropped from a high of 54 percent in 1977 to 34.5 percent in 2006, according to NORC, and the percentage of Americans who reported personally owning a gun has shrunk to just under 22 percent.

So, by the rules of democratic play, one might assume that the majority would have major influence on legislation. But that's not how it works, thanks to the enormous influence of the gun lobby. The gun lobby's stranglehold on reform and preventing gun violence can best be summarized as a "tyranny of the smallest minority" of gun extremists. Poll after poll demonstrate that even among gun owners, overwhelming numbers of Americans support stronger laws to reduce and prevent gun violence.

The long-term decline monitored by the Chicago survey has buoyed proponents of tighter gun controls. "America's gun culture is fading," says Josh Sugarmann, who heads the Washington-based Violence Policy Center.

According to Sugarmann, those keeping the culture alive and those most vocal in resisting tighter regulations are white, middle-aged men whose enthusiasm for firearms, hunting and shooting is not shared by younger Americans. Yet, at the moment it's difficult to imagine the U.S. without its gun culture. . . .

Fewer People Have More Guns

Gun rampages happen with such numbing regularity—on average one every three weeks in 2007—that they barely make news unless the death toll climbs into double digits, as happened at the Virginia Tech university [in Blacksburg, Virginia]. There, a student with mental problems killed 32 of his peers and himself.

President George W. Bush [in January 2008] signed into law a bill meant to prevent people with a record of mental disease from buying weapons.

Virginia Tech was the worst school shooting in U.S. history and rekindled the debate over the easy availability of guns in America. There are more private firearms in the United States than anywhere else in the world—at least 200 million. While that arsenal has been growing every year, the proportion of U.S. households where guns are held has been shrinking. In other words: Fewer people have more guns. One estimate, by the National Police Foundation, says that 10 percent of the country's adults own roughly three quarters of all firearms.

Towards a Sane Gun Policy

How do we break America's obsession with "gun culture"? Well one possibility is that as the NORC survey noted, as fewer Americans own guns, the "gun vote" will continue to decrease and play a smaller role in our politics, especially on statewide and national elections. And again, gun owners are already a small and diminishing minority.

Over time Americans will look for pragmatic solutions from our leaders to save lives and reduce gun violence.

There are several other tactics. Local, state and grassroots driven victories for gun violence prevention measures will begin to crack the gun lobby's monopoly on the policy debate over guns. Perhaps most importantly, elected officials need to stand up to the gun lobby and not shirk away from taking gun extremists on. The truth is that the gun lobby is hardly the powerful entity that people think they are. The NRA [National Rifle Association] is in large part a paper tiger.

As our recent presidential caucuses and primaries have shown, authenticity matters most. Political candidates and advocates for gun control can win hearts and minds simply by taking the gun lobby on strongly, demonstrating their courage and dismissing special-interest politics epitomized by the gun lobby.

Is America's gun culture fading? Absolutely. It will not happen overnight, and this is certainly a longterm fight. But over time the extremist elements of the gun lobby will start losing to rational voices. Over time Americans will look for pragmatic solutions from our leaders to save lives and reduce gun violence, rather than coddle up to the gun lobby's radical agenda. It's not hope or wishful thinking that leads us to this conclusion. The trending and data are pointing America to a just and sane policy over guns in our country.

The Media Show an Anti-Gun Bias in Reporting Gun Violence

David Niedrauer

David Niedrauer is a former intern at the Culture and Media Institute, an organization dedicated to promoting fair coverage of social and religious conservative views in the media.

When it comes to the right to bear arms—to accept personal responsibility to defend home and family—the media are far from fair and balanced. During the first seven months of 2007, the media waged an intermittent war against the Second Amendment [of the Constitution: the right to bear arms], using a variety of fallacious arguments to make the pitch for gun control. This . . . report will begin by detailing what the media reported on gun issues, and then point out essential information the media failed to mention.

The Media Assault

A crime wave in the big cities, followed by the Virginia Tech tragedy in April [2007, in which 32 people were killed by a lone gunman], gave the media plenty of ammunition for attacking the right to bear arms. The three major broadcast networks ran at least 650 stories on gun homicides from January through July. In a manner reminiscent of [leftwing documentarist] Michael Moore, journalists sprinkled post-Virginia Tech news coverage with comparisons between the United States and other countries that have stricter gun control laws and less crime.

The media first broached the urban crime wave immediately following a March 9 court decision, *Parker v. District of*

David Niedrauer, "The Media Assault on the Second Amendment," *Eye on Culture*, Vol. 1, No. 11, August 27, 2007. Reproduced by permission of the Culture and Media Institute, a division of the Media Research Center.

Columbia, which struck down D.C.'s handgun ban. ABC, NBC, CNN, the *New York Times*, the *Washington Post*, and *USA Today* each ran at least one story on the crime wave between March 9 and March 29 [2007].

The Virginia Tech shootings . . . allowed the media to accelerate massively their campaign against the Second Amendment.

On the March 10 [2007] NBC *Nightly News*, anchor John Seigenthaler tried to link the crime wave and the decision: "A new study of major cities shows an alarming rise in violence. . . . This comes on the heels of a federal court decision striking down a gun control law in Washington, D.C., on the grounds it violated the constitutional right to bear arms." A major problem: Seigenthaler failed to acknowledge that the D.C. gun ban was in effect while the crime wave was taking place.

Many media outlets recycled the crime wave story to bash guns again later in the year. For example, on July 8 [2007], ABC *World News Sunday* ran a piece on the crime wave, focusing on Philadelphia. ABC anchor Dan Harris laid blame for Philadelphia's crime problem at the feet of "rural lawmakers" in Pennsylvania who support Second Amendment rights. While "rural sensibilities continue to rule the gun debate," said reporter David Kerley, "cities like Philadelphia prepare for another night and another shooting death."

From July 24 through July 26 [2007], CBS *Evening News* ran a three-part series called *Battle Line: Philadelphia*, which blamed guns and a shortage of government anti-poverty spending for criminal activity in the inner city. CBS quoted numerous gun control advocates like Miami Chief of Police John Timoney: "[T]here's been no national effort to deal with this—with the guns and the availability of guns, and any reasonable measures that have been advocated have been defeated by Congress." CBS failed to report that police chiefs who support gun control are in the minority. A 2005 survey by the National Association of Chiefs of Police found that 93.6 percent of chiefs and sheriffs support "civilian gun ownership rights," and 63.1 percent claimed that concealed-weapons permits reduce violent crime. Not surprisingly, the same survey reports that 93.2 percent say the news media is "not fair and balanced."

The Virginia Tech shootings on April 16 [2007] allowed the media to accelerate massively their campaign against the Second Amendment. Journalists would eventually demonstrate their willingness to smear their own country in order to promote gun control. Just as Michael Moore, in his movie *Sicko*, excoriated America's private healthcare system by inaccurately comparing it to socialized medicine in other countries, journalists blasted America's constitutional right to bear arms by pointing to countries that have stricter gun laws and less crime.

On the day of the Virginia Tech tragedy, Armen Keteyian of CBS *Evening News* used an anti-gun lobby's rating as the standard by which to assess Virginia: "[the state] recently earned a C minus rating by the Brady Center to Prevent Gun Violence."

The embattled university, Keteyian asserted, has desperately fought Virginia's "hunting culture" in order to "safeguard the student population."

NBC anchor Brian Williams heaped praise on Britain's gun ban on the April 17 *Nightly News*: "Britain outlawed handguns, and anyone caught with one faces a minimum prison sentence of five years. They are so opposed to guns here that not even police officers on routine patrol carry them. Now gun violence is rare." Williams ignored several salient facts: by tradition, British "bobbies" have rarely carried firearms; Britain has a growing problem with knife violence; and other nations where gun ownership is common enjoy low rates of gun violence. For example, Switzerland, which has very low crime rates, actually issues assault rifles to all adult males for militia service.

In their zeal to repeal the Second Amendment, the media failed to inform their audience of at least four powerful arguments against gun control.

Two days after the Virginia Tech massacre, the *Washington Post* was also taking lines from the Michael Moore playbook, attacking not only the Second Amendment, but American foreign policy. Nations around the world, reported the *Post*, "used the university attack to condemn what they depicted as U.S. policies to arm friends, attack enemies and rely on violence rather than dialogue to settle disputes."

The *New York Times* took aim at a target closer to home. "It is the gun lobby's incessant efforts to weaken the gun laws that make a tragedy like the one at Virginia Tech possible," screeched the Gray Lady [as the *New York Times* is often called] in an April 26 [2007] editorial.

The Media's Omissions

In their zeal to repeal the Second Amendment, the media failed to inform their audience of at least four powerful arguments against gun control.

1. Comparisons between countries are not useful. Unfortunately, direct comparisons between countries based solely on crime rates and gun laws tell very little about whether gun control actually works. Social scientists believe that gun control is only one of many factors that influence rates of violence.

The National Academy of Sciences cautioned in a 2004 report, *Firearms and Violence: A Critical Review*, that, "It is difficult to gauge the value of [gun control] measures because social and economic factors behind criminal acts are often complex and interwoven, and the efforts are narrow in scope."

The media almost completely failed to report on an issue most relevant to the Second Amendment debate: the legitimate use of guns in self defense.

As Brian Williams compared the U.S. and Britain to promote gun control, a pro-gun analyst could easily cherry pick countries to "prove" that gun control doesn't work. New Zealand, with very limited gun restrictions, has an annual gun homicide rate of 0.18 per 100,000 population. South Africa, where the Firearm Control Act of 2000 licenses firearms to virtually no one, has a rate of 74.57.

A 1998 Library of Congress report concluded, "From available statistics, among 27 countries surveyed, it is difficult to find a correlation between the existence of strict firearms regulations and a lower incidence of gun-related crimes."

2. Guns are frequently used to stop crimes. Between January 1 and August 1 [2007] the media almost completely failed to report on an issue most relevant to the Second Amendment debate: the legitimate use of guns in self defense. To the Founding Fathers, the right to bear arms for self protection was essential if citizens were to be truly free. Alexander Hamilton addressed the "original right of self defense" in *Federalist 28* [the *Federalist Papers* were a series of articles discussing the proposed Constitution of the United States]. Under a "confederacy" that protects the right to bear arms, wrote Hamilton, "the people, without exaggeration, may be said to be entirely the masters of their own fate." In other words, to have the ability to accept responsibility for defending themselves, rather than having to rely exclusively on the government. Hamilton knew what he was talking about: guns are often used to stop criminals. According to a 1997 survey by the United States *Journal of Criminal Law*, more than 2.5 million people use a gun in self defense each year.

This essential fact never saw the light of day in the mainstream media. From January through July, armed self defense almost never made it into the news. While the three major TV networks broadcast at least 650 stories about gun homicides, CMI [Culture and Media Institute] was able to find only two stories about guns used by citizens to defend themselves. John Stossel, anchor of ABC's *20/20*, referred to two cases of armed self defense on the May 4 show. NBC's *Today* show of April 23 [2007] featured former Miss America Venus Ramey, 82, who chased an intruder off her property with a shotgun.

At worst, gun control laws leave law-abiding citizens defenseless before rapacious criminals, and at best, they may not affect violence at all.

The major networks also failed to mention a highly relevant incident, the 2002 shooting at the Appalachian School of Law in Grundy, Virginia. After killing three people, a gunman was forced to surrender by two armed students. Virginia Tech, in contrast, did not allow students to be armed, so nobody was able to stop Seung-Hui Cho on that fateful day in Norris Hall.

3. Most guns used in crimes are illegally acquired. Like it or not, banning guns only takes them out of the hands of law-abiding citizens, making it easier for people with no respect for the law to attack their victims. The National Academy of Sciences concluded in its report, *Firearms and Violence*, that only 21 percent of the guns used to commit crimes in this country are bought legally. In countries with strict gun control laws, the proportion can drop well below 10 percent. Legally purchased guns are rarely used to commit crimes, but every time a gun ban is passed, responsible citizens lose the capacity to defend themselves and their families.

4. Gun control laws have no proven effect. At worst, gun control laws leave law-abiding citizens defenseless before rapacious criminals, and at best, they may not affect violence at all.

The *Firearms and Violence* study surveyed local gun control policies around the nation, including more than 80 education programs designed to prevent violence in children, but could not find any that actually reduced gun violence.

The U.S. Centers for Disease Control and Prevention published one of the most comprehensive surveys of gun control laws ever in 2003. The survey looked at bans on firearms, restrictions on firearms, waiting periods and licensing, zero tolerance laws in schools, childhood access prevention laws and combinations of all of these. The result? "The Task Force found insufficient evidence to determine the effectiveness of any of the firearms laws or combinations of laws reviewed on violent outcomes."

Why do the media repeatedly make the same faulty assumptions and advance the same shopworn arguments for expensive and intrusive gun control policies that have no proven effect on crime, and render law-abiding citizens helpless to defend themselves? In a word, ideology. The argument for gun control has always been based more on utopian visions than empirical facts. That, and the left simply does not trust an armed citizenry. The media's incessant attacks on the Second Amendment demonstrate clearly their liberal bias against gun ownership.

CHAPTER 2

Can Gun Control Measures Reduce Gun Violence?

Chapter Overview

William J. Krouse

William J. Krouse is an analyst in the Domestic Social Policy division of the Congressional Research Service, part of the Library of Congress.

Congress continues to debate the efficacy and constitutionality of federal regulation of firearms and ammunition. It is a contentious debate, with strong advocates for and against the further federal regulation of firearms.

Gun control advocates argue that federal regulation of firearms curbs access by criminals, juveniles, and other "high-risk" individuals. They contend that only federal measures can successfully reduce the availability of guns throughout the nation. Some seek broad policy changes such as near-prohibition of non-police handgun ownership or the registration of all firearms or firearm owners. They assert that there is no constitutional barrier to such measures and no significant social costs. Others advocate less comprehensive policies that they maintain would not impede ownership and legitimate firearm transfers.

Gun control opponents deny that federal policies keep firearms out of the hands of high-risk persons; rather, they argue, controls often create burdens for law-abiding citizens and infringe upon constitutional rights provided by the Second Amendment. Some argue further that widespread gun ownership is one of the best deterrents to crime as well as to potential tyranny, whether by gangs or by government. They may also criticize the notion of enhancing federal, as opposed to state, police powers. . . .

Through the years, legislative proposals to restrict the availability of firearms to the public have raised the following

William J. Krouse, "Gun Control in the 108th Congress," *Congressional Research Service*, May 6, 2005, p. 9.

questions: What restrictions on firearms are permissible under the Constitution? Does gun control constitute crime control? Can the nation's rates of homicide, robbery, and assault be reduced by the stricter regulation of firearm commerce or ownership? Would restrictions stop attacks on public figures or thwart deranged persons and terrorists? Would household, street corner, and schoolyard disputes be less lethal if firearms were more difficult and expensive to acquire? Would more restrictive gun control policies have the unintended effect of impairing citizens' means of self-defense?

Gun control opponents . . . insist on the continuing need of people for effective means to defend person and property.

The Pro/Con Debate

In recent years, proponents of gun control legislation have often held that only *federal* laws can be effective in the United States. Otherwise, they say, states with few restrictions will continue to be sources of guns that flow illegally into more restrictive states. They believe that the Second Amendment to the Constitution, which states that "A well regulated Militia, being necessary to the security of a free State, the right of the people to keep and bear Arms shall not be infringed," is being misread in today's modern society. They argue that the Second Amendment: (1) is now obsolete, with the presence of professional police forces; (2) was intended solely to guard against suppression of state militias by the central government and therefore restricted in scope by that intent; or (3) does not guarantee a right that is absolute, but one that can be limited by reasonable requirements. They ask why a private citizen needs any firearm in today's modern society that is not designed primarily for hunting or other recognized sporting purposes.

Proponents of firearm restrictions have advocated policy changes on specific types of firearms or components that they feel are useful primarily for criminal purposes or that pose unusual risks to the public. Fully automatic firearms (i.e., machine guns) and short-barreled rifles and shotguns have been subject to strict regulation since 1934. Fully automatic firearms have been banned from private possession since 1986, except for those legally owned and registered with the Secretary of the Treasury on [or before] May 19, 1986. More recently, "Saturday night specials" (loosely defined as inexpensive, small handguns), "assault weapons," ammunition-feeding devices with capacities for more than seven rounds, and certain ammunition have been the focus of control efforts.

Opponents of gun control vary in their positions with respect to specific forms of control but generally hold that gun control laws do not accomplish what is intended. They argue that it is as difficult to keep weapons from being acquired by "high risk" individuals, even under federal laws and enforcement, as it was . . . to stop the sale and use of liquor during Prohibition. In their view, a more stringent federal firearm regulatory system would only create problems for law-abiding citizens, bring mounting frustration and escalation of bans by gun regulators, and possibly threaten citizens' civil rights or safety. Some argue that the low violent crime rates of other countries have nothing to do with gun control, maintaining instead that multiple cultural differences are responsible.

Gun control opponents also reject the assumption that the only legitimate purpose of ownership by a private citizen is recreational (i.e., hunting and target-shooting). They insist on the continuing need of people for effective means to defend person and property, and they point to studies that they believe show that gun possession lowers the incidence of crime. They say that the law enforcement and criminal justice system in the United States has not demonstrated the ability to furnish an adequate measure of public safety in all settings. Some opponents believe further that the Second Amendment includes a right to keep arms as a defense against potential government tyranny, pointing to examples in other countries of the use of firearm restrictions to curb dissent and secure illegitimate government power.

The debate has been intense. To gun control advocates, the opposition is out of touch with the times, misinterprets the Second Amendment, or is lacking in concern for the problems of crime and violence. To gun control opponents, advocates are naive in their faith in the power of regulation to solve social problems, bent on disarming the American citizen for ideological or social reasons, or moved by irrational hostility to firearms and gun enthusiasts.

Gun-Related Statistics

Crime and mortality statistics are often used in the gun control debate. According to a recent study, however, none of the existing sources of statistics provide either comprehensive, timely, or accurate data with which to definitively assess whether there is a causal connection between firearms and violence. For example, existing data do not show whether the number of people shot and killed with semiautomatic assault weapons declined during the 10-year period (1994–2004) those firearms were banned from further proliferation in the United States. Presented below are data on the following topics: (1) the number of guns in the United States, (2) firearm-related homicides, (3) non-lethal/firearm-related victimizations, (4) gun violence and youth, (5) gun-related mortality rates, (6) use of firearms for personal defense, and (7) recreational use of firearms. In some cases, the data presented below are over a decade old, but remain the most recent available.

How Many Guns Are in the United States? The National Institute of Justice (NIJ) reported in a national survey that in 1994, 44 million people, approximately 35% of households, owned 192 million firearms, 65 million of which were handguns. Seventy-four percent of those individuals were reported to own more than one firearm. According to Bureau of Alcohol, Tobacco, and Firearms (ATF), by the end of 1996 approximately 242 million firearms were available for sale to or were possessed by civilians in the United States. That total includes roughly 72 million handguns (mostly pistols, revolvers, and derringers), 76 million rifles, and 64 million shotguns. By 2000, the number of firearms had increased to approximately 259 million: 92 million handguns, 92 million rifles, and 75 million shotguns.

Most guns available for sale are produced domestically. In recent years, 1 to 2 million handguns were manufactured each year, along with 1 million rifles and fewer than 1 million shotguns. Annual imports are considerably smaller—from 200,000 to 400,000 handguns, 200,000 rifles, and 100,000 to 200,000 shotguns. Retail prices of guns vary widely, from $75 or less for inexpensive, low-caliber handguns to more than $1,500 for higher-end standard-production rifles or shotguns. Data are not available on the number of "assault weapons" in private possession or available for sale, but one study estimated that there were 1.5 million privately owned assault weapons in 1994.

How Often Are Guns Used in Homicides? Reports submitted by state and local law enforcement agencies to the Federal Bureau of Investigation (FBI) and published annually in the *Uniform Crime Reports* indicate that the violent crime rate has declined from 1981 through 2003; however, the number of homicides and the proportion involving firearms have increased in recent years. From 1993 to 1999, the number of firearm-related homicides decreased by an average rate of nearly 11% annually, for an overall decrease of 49%. Since then, firearm-related homicides have *increased*:

- by 2% (to 8,661) in 2000;

- by 2.6% (to 8,890) in 2001;

- by 7.2% (to 9,528) in 2002; and

- by 1.2% (to 9,638) in 2003 (according to preliminary data).

In addition, of homicides in which the type of weapon could be identified, from 60% to almost 70% have involved firearms each year. In 2002, of the 14,263 homicides reported, 67% (9,528) were committed with firearms. Of those committed with firearms, 77% (7,294) involved handguns.

How Often Are Guns Used in Non-lethal Crimes? The other principal source of national crime data is the *National Crime Victimization Survey* (NCVS) conducted by the Bureau of the Census and published by the Bureau of Justice Statistics (BJS). The NCVS database provides some information on the weapons used by offenders, based on victims' reports. Based on data provided by survey respondents in calendar year 2003, BJS estimated that, nationwide, there were 5.4 million violent crimes (rape or sexual assault, robbery, aggravated assault, and simple assault). Weapons were used in about 1.2 million of these criminal incidents. Firearms were used by offenders in about 367,000 of these incidents, or roughly 7%.

How Prevalent Is Gun Violence Among Youth? Youth crime statistics have often been used in the gun control debate. The number of homicides committed annually with a firearm by persons in the 14- to 24-year-old age group increased sharply from 1985 to 1993; they have declined since then, but not returned to the 1985 level. According to the BJS, from 1985 to 1993, the number of firearm-related homicides committed by 14- to 17-year-olds increased by 294%, from 855 to 3,371. From 1993 to 2000, the number of firearm-related homicides committed by persons in this age group decreased by 68%, from 3,371 to 1,084. From 1985 to 1993, firearm-related homicides committed by 18- to 24-year-olds increased by 142%, from 3,374 to 8,171. From 1993 to 1999. firearm-related homicides committed by persons in this age group decreased by 39%, from 8,171 to 4,988. They increased by 3% to 5,162 in 2000. More recent statistics for youth have yet to be reported. Although gun-related violence in schools is statistically a rare event, a Department of Justice survey indicated that 12% of students age 12 to 19 reported knowing a student who brought a firearm to school.

How Prevalent Are Gun-Related Fatalities? Firearm fatalities have decreased continuously from 1993 through 2001. The source of national data on firearm deaths is the publication *Vital Statistics*, published each year by the National Center for Health Statistics. Firearm deaths reported by coroners in each state are presented in four categories: homicides and legal intervention [e.g., police], suicides, accidents, and unknown circumstances. In 2002, a total of 30,242 firearm deaths occurred, according to such reports. Of this total, 12,129 were homicides or due to legal intervention; 17,108 were suicides: 762 were unintentional (accidental) shootings; and 243 were of unknown cause. From 1993 to 2000, firearm-related deaths decreased by an average rate of nearly 5% annually, for an overall decrease of nearly 28%. As compared to 2000, firearm deaths increased by 3% in 2001. They increased again by 2% in 2002. Also in 2002, there were 1,443 juvenile (under 18 years of age) deaths attributed to firearms. Of the juvenile total, 879 were homicides or due to legal intervention; 423 were suicides; 115 were unintentional; and 26 were of unknown cause. From 1993 to 2001, firearm-related deaths for juveniles have decreased by an average rate of 10% annually, for an overall decrease of 56%. As compared to 2001, they increased slightly in . . . 2002, by less than 1%.

How Often Are Firearms Used in Self-Defense? According to BJS, NCVS data from 1987 to 1992 indicate that in each of those years roughly 62,200 victims of violent crime (1% of all victims of such crimes) used guns to defend themselves. Another 20,000 persons each year used guns to protect property.

Persons in the business of self-protection (police officers, armed security guards) may have been included in the survey. Another source of information on the use of firearms for self-defense is the "National Self Defense Survey" conducted by criminology professor Gary Kleck of Florida State University in the spring of 1993. Citing responses from 4,978 households, Dr. Kleck estimated that handguns have been used 2.1 million times per year for self-defense, and that all types of guns have been used approximately 2.5 million times a year for that purpose during the 1988-1993 period.

Why do these numbers vary by such a wide margin? Law enforcement agencies do not collect information on the number of times civilians use firearms to defend themselves or their property against attack. Such data have been collected in household surveys. The contradictory nature of the available statistics may be partially explained by methodological factors. That is, these and other criminal justice statistics reflect what is *reported* to have occurred, not necessarily the actual number of times certain events occur. Victims and offenders are sometimes reluctant to be candid with researchers. So, the number of incidents can only be estimated, making it difficult to state with certainty the accuracy of statistics such as the number of times firearms are used in self-defense. For this and other reasons, criminal justice statistics often vary when different methodologies are applied.

Survey research can be limited, since it is difficult to produce statistically significant findings from small incident populations. For example, the sample in the National Self-Defense Survey might have been too small, given the likely low incidence rate and the inherent limitations of survey research.

What About the Recreational Use of Guns? According to NIJ, in 1994 recreation was the most common motivation for owning a firearm. There were approximately 15 million hunters, about 35% of gun owners, in the United States and about the same number and percentage of gun owners engaged in sport shooting in 1994. More recently, the U.S. Fish and Wildlife Service reported that there were over 14.7 million persons who were paid license holders in 2003 and, according to the National Shooting Sports Foundation in that year approximately 15.2 million persons hunted with a firearm and nearly 19.8 million participated in target shooting.

Federal Laws Are Needed to Reduce Gun Violence

John Rosenthal

John Rosenthal is a real estate developer in Massachusetts, a gun owner, and founder of a gun control advocacy organization called Stop Handgun Violence.

Given the virtually unregulated access to guns in the US, it's actually surprising that there aren't more than 80–90 gun deaths and 200–300 injuries everyday. There are an average of 30,000 gun deaths and 100,000 gun injuries each year. The average US annual firearm fatality rate is 10.6 per 100,000 population which is more than the entire industrialized world combined. Since 1999 when the US experienced a 30 year low in violent crime, most US cities have experienced a dramatic increase in gun violence. The difference between then and now is that the gun lobby now dictates national gun policy, and the deadly trend will continue until the President and Congress enact a handful of effective uniform national gun laws that address the unrestricted private sale of guns, including at 5,000 gun shows without even a criminal background check, support rather than restrict law enforcement, and confront race, poverty and the lack of economic opportunity in our poorest neighborhoods.

The Availability of Guns

For instance, although Massachusetts has enacted the most effective gun violence prevention laws and initiatives in the country and is among the top three states with the lowest firearm fatality rate in the US, it is an island surrounded by a sea of states where criminals can buy and sell an unlimited number of guns without even an ID or background check. To make matters worse in the last seven years the Federal government has not only turned a blind eye towards gun violence it has intentionally allowed easy access to guns and restricted law enforcement's ability to prevent and prosecute criminals who use and traffic guns. In fact there aren't even Federal minimum mandatory gun trafficking statutes on the books and incredibly, the US Justice Department requires that the FBI destroy National Instant Check (NICS) gun purchase records after 24 hours making it nearly impossible for police to track gun traffickers and illegal multiple gun sale patterns. The primary reason is the NRA [National Rifle Association] and gun lobby's influence and control over Congress and the [George W.] Bush administration. As a result the Federal Government renders nearly useless what few national gun laws that do exist and sadly law enforcement is unnecessarily put at risk by easy criminal access to much more powerful military style weapons and ammunition than police are issued to protect themselves and the public.

The solutions to gun violence are relatively simple—it's the politics that stand in the way of saving lives from largely preventable gun violence.

According to law enforcement, crime guns are coming from the following sources:

1. Home, car, and gun dealer invasions/break-ins and subsequent undocumented "secondary sale" transfers.

2. Straw purchasers (buyers with clean background checks) who lawfully purchase guns from FFL's [dealers with a federal firearm license] as well as private sellers and then resell to anyone without a background check requirement or documentation. Historically about 1 percent of FFL's are responsible for approximately 60% of guns traced to crimes.

3. Gun shows, flea markets and other "secondary sale" markets in the 32 states where no background checks or documentation is required. There are over 5,000 gun shows in the US each year where over half the guns sold are transferred by "private sellers." In addition the Bureau of Alcohol Tobacco Firearms and Explosives (BATF) is literally prohibited from regulating "private sales" especially at "politically radioactive" gun shows and flea markets.

Solutions

So what's the answer to gun violence in the US?

1. Enact uniform national gun laws similar to what has worked in Massachusetts that:

- Require background checks for *all* gun purchases including for "private sales" and especially at gun shows, and flea markets

- Require safe storage of all firearms unless they are in the owner's direct control to reduce guns from home, car and dealer theft

- Allow the FBI to maintain gun purchase records and include criminal *and* mental health history that can be accessed by gun dealers and law enforcement

- Develop effective federal gun trafficking laws with minimum mandatory sentences for unlawful multiple gun sales

- Create incentives for gun manufacturers to produce "personalized" and "child-proof" guns that only the intended user can fire

2. Create economic opportunities, job training, mentoring programs and close the equality and social "equity" gap for the geographically small and disproportionately dangerous and poor urban neighborhoods where virtually all the gun violence and gang activity takes place.

Political Obstacles

The solutions to gun violence are relatively simple—it's the politics that stand in the way of saving lives from largely preventable gun violence: reduce easy access to guns by kids, the mentally ill and criminals with uniform national laws, support vs. restrict law enforcement's ability to enforce gun laws and acknowledge and address the realities of poverty, race and social inequity in especially our inner city neighborhoods, schools and employment sectors.

Unfortunately these solutions require the political will and courage to stand up to the greed, ignorance and shortsightedness of the gun lobby and their supporters in Congress and the White House. We must recognize that if gun violence were killing mostly suburban white kids like at Virginia Tech, Columbine High, University of Texas, Jonesboro Elementary School or Anyboro USA vs. the 80–90 mostly urban kids of color everyday, the uproar ... would be deafening and Congress and the President would act. It's way past the time for the uproar to quiet the sound of gunshots in the United States- gun violence capital of the world!

Congress Must Enact Strict Gun Control Laws

Jeff Kirvin

Jeff Kirvin keeps a blog, JeffKirvin.net.

Okay, I've waited a "decent interval" after the [2007] Virginia Tech [university in Blacksburg, Virginia] shootings to bring this up. But now that we've had yet another horrific incident of gun violence in this country, isn't it about time we start talking seriously about gun control?

I know the NRA [National Rifle Association, a pro-gun advocacy group] would love it if the public followed the lead of our politicians and remained silent on this matter. It drove me nuts that in the wake of the VT [Virginia Tech] shootings Republicans and Democrats alike seemed to act like talking about the "gun" part of gun violence was a taboo subject. But the fact remains, you can't have gun violence without the guns, and frankly, the United States has a heavily armed monkey on its back.

Guns and Gun Violence

Fact: Having a gun in your home makes it over 20 times more likely that it will be used to kill someone you know than any other gun.

On average, we've had a major gun-related mass murder in this country every 18 months for the last 30 years. That's not a few isolated wackos, that's a trend. A consistent trend. And it's something we could address if we really wanted to and weren't so sure that even discussing the idea of restricting handguns was political suicide.

No Constitutional Barriers to Gun Control

It doesn't have to be this way. Contrary to popular belief, the Second Amendment of the United States Constitution doesn't say "guns for all." Here's what it says, actually.

> A well regulated militia, being necessary to the security of a free state, the right of the people to keep and bear arms, shall not be infringed.

See that? "Well regulated militia." Nowhere does the Second Amendment protect the rights of civilians to keep weapons. Only members of the militia are so protected so that they, in turn, can maintain the security of the state. Today, we call that militia by two names: the National Guard and the Army. They have outfits and everything. And they have guns. Lots of them.

But the rest of us don't need them, or we shouldn't. When the Bill of Rights [containing the Second Amendment] was written, the United States had no standing army and it was expected that citizens would rise up and fight for their country when needed, much like the Swiss are today. As soon as we formed a standing army, the Second Amendment was obsolete, and should draw no more attention today than other parts of the Constitution that are irrelevant and out of date.

As for the oft-cited idea that we have to have an armed populace to prevent governmental oppression, two questions:

1. See those "free speech zones" that pop up whenever Bush speaks? How's that fight against governmental oppression going?

2. Does it really matter if you have an AR-15 or a handgun when the government has tanks? See Square, Tiananmen [on June 4, 1984, the Chinese army fired on unarmed protesters there, killing hundreds].

So guns are a problem, and the Constitution doesn't actually say that civilians are allowed to be armed to the teeth. Now what?

"If bullets cost $5,000 each, there would be no innocent by-standers." —[Comedian] Chris Rock

Well, I have some ideas on how we can actually curb gun violence in this country. None involve door to door searches by jack-booted thugs come to take your guns, and all could be done by a willing Congress.

Ideas for Curbing Gun Violence

Tax ammunition. The first and easiest thing to do would make bullets much, much more expensive, and then use the tax dollars from the sale of bullets to fund programs for the victims of gun violence. Nice poetic justice there. I'm not talking about the $5,000 per bullet joked about by Chris Rock, but something along the lines of $50 a bullet would make firing off a bunch of rounds a much more daunting and expensive proposition. Law enforcement would obviously be exempted from this tax.

Restrict the sale of "non-sport" automatic weapons to law enforcement. This one is a little more ballsy. Congress can and should enact legislation that would make it illegal to sell handguns or assault weapons to people without the proper law enforcement or security credentials. Regular civilians could still buy shotguns and hunting rifles under the same rules we have today, but you don't need a Glock or an AR-15 to hunt.

Civilian access to automatic ballistic weapons is a threat to national security.

Melt guns used in crimes. This one sounds like a no-brainer, but not all municipalities do this. Some places wholesale the guns and they wind up back out on the market. This is frankly inexcusable and I can't believe it still goes on. If a gun is used in the commission or attempt of a crime, it should be destroyed, never to be used by anyone again.

Step up prosecution of illegal gun running. As far as I'm concerned, we could take all the cops currently working narcotics and move them to gun trafficking and end up with a safer populace. This will be needed especially once handguns become illegal to sell to ordinary civilians. Over time, the supply of guns won't stop but it will thin significantly.

> Fact: Countries like Japan and the EU [European Union] which have much stricter gun laws than we do have far, far lower incidence of gun violence.

This is a hard problem and it can't be solved overnight, but that doesn't mean we shouldn't try. If we're really serious about this "homeland security" idea that means making our streets safer from bad people among our own population as well as the countless gun-related accidental deaths we suffer every year.

Civilian access to automatic ballistic weapons is a threat to national security. Period. It's time to do something to make us all safer.

Raising the Tax on Firearms May Reduce Gun Violence

Kent Garry

Kent Garry is a public school geography teacher and a former lieutenant colonel of the United States Army who lives in Texas.

In light of the campus killings of twenty at Northern Illinois State University [in February 2008], the Kirkwood, Missouri City Council killing of five the week before, and the Virginia Tech campus massacre of thirty-three [April 2007], perhaps it's time for America to revisit the issue of gun control.

Truly, here in the Dallas [Texas] area it seems like there is at least one senseless shooting tragedy in the news every day . . . kids robbing convenience stores and killing proprietors who resist, others blindly shooting through curtained windows of homes hitting innocent women and children. Hardly ever do we hear about citizens legitimately defending themselves, their families or property with guns; notwithstanding, many Americans feel that they need guns for self-protection. The number of states with some version of a Concealed Carry law, either "shall issue" or "not restricted" has grown from nine in 1986 to thirty-nine today. All the remaining states are currently considering concealed carry laws. Clearly, America's response to increasing gun violence has been to arm itself. . . .

The Swiss Example

[An e-mail acquaintance responded to my call for gun control, saying] "I suspect . . . that you would favor a more restrictive government policy toward gun ownership. If this is true, are you sure that there is a cause and effect relationship between gun ownership and violent crime? How is it that our

Kent Garry, "Gun Violence—Why It's Not a Political Issue This Time Around, Not Yet Anyway," *The World According to Opa*, February 23, 2008. Reproduced by permission.

good friends, the Swiss, who have firearms (military firearms with ample supplies of ammunition) in virtually every home in the land, who carry firearms openly in the streets and on public transportation without public alarm, who participate in shooting sports like we play golf, have virtually no gun crime, allow their children to walk or ride public transportation to school unescorted, and can walk the streets of their cities day or night without fear of harm? Are guns really the root of our violent crime problem or could it be something else?"

This lady concluded her response by suggesting that we will likely hear nothing about gun-control debated in this election year [2008] because it is such a divisive political issue. I wrote back saying, "I'm not so sure that you are right about our not hearing anything from the candidates about gun control prior to the November elections. The Supreme Court has agreed to relook the question of whether the Second Amendment is still relevant to 'individual' ownership of guns. They are doing so in response to an appeal associated with Washington D.C.'s legal attempts to limit gun crime in that city.... A decision is expected by June [2008]. Results in this case either way are, I think, likely to make gun control an issue for debate by Presidential and Congressional candidates ... whether they want the debate or not."

Until we are able to close the many social/economic gaps in our country that spawn violent crime, ... [gun control] should be put back on the legislative agenda.

I went on to say, "Compared to Americans, the Swiss are a very different people. They're different in many ways. They're better educated for one thing, and they have no recent history of war. They have a higher per capita GDP [gross domestic product, a measure of a country's economic output] than other larger European countries, Japan, or even the U.S. The distribution of wealth in Switzerland is much more equitable than here in the U.S., and the crime rate is much, much lower. Although they speak many different languages, they have never had a "civil rights" issue with large segments of their society being treated as inferior citizens, and they control their borders. Their unemployment rate is currently less than one fourth of ours too.

"Unlike here in the U.S., the Swiss still employ militia as a large part of their self defense forces. This explains for me why personal firearms are so prevalent there. We used to rely on militias for national defense too, which was the original basis/justification for the Second Amendment. Since we no longer rely on militias, those of us on my side of the gun argument wonder how our counterparts rationalize that it still applies.

"Rather than comparing us to the Swiss as an argument against gun control, why not consider our closer neighbors for a comparison, the Canadians, as an argument for gun control? We've a lot more in common with them—historically, socially, economically. Murders committed with firearms per capita have been more than eight times higher in recent years here in the U.S. than in Canada. Murder by other means (without guns) has been almost twice as high. This, in my mind, clearly establishes a correlation between guns and violent crime."

Let's Put Gun Control Back on the Legislative Agenda

So, until we are able to close the many social/economic gaps in our country that spawn violent crime, I truly do think that limiting the proliferation of guns and access to them by convicted felons and mental patients should be put back on the legislative agenda. I would personally feel much safer knowing that there are not more hand guns in this country than people who might use them.

Once the Second Amendment question is resolved this summer [2008] by the Supreme Court, states and local governments may be free to decide appropriate ownership and use restrictions.[1] Then enforcement becomes a nightmare, right? So, instead of local, unenforceable laws, perhaps the following would work to reduce the number of hand guns and, therefore, the violence perpetrated with them: levying a heavy federally-mandated sales tax on new, legal purchases coupled with annual property/ownership/use taxes; putting some real teeth into a national registry database and allowing sellers to be sued for not properly employing it, and; instituting a buy-back program for weapons such as our Australian friends have done. The last measure in this list could be paid for with revenue received from new hand-gun manufacturing taxes and an excise tax on imported hand guns.

Shot guns and hunting rifles? These have legitimate uses by sportsmen and women. But what to do about assault guns (fully automatic rifles and machine pistols), that's a whole 'nuther matter. These, I believe, as well as all armor piercing ammunition, must be outlawed for private ownership at the Federal level.

Suggesting these things won't make my gun-loving friends happy with me, I know. But then, I'm not running for public office.

---

1. On June 26, 2008, the Supreme Court found in *District of Columbia v. Heller* that the Second Amendment protects an individual's right to possess a firearm for private use.

The United States Must Promote Responsible Access and Use of Guns

Richard H. Brodhead and James Moeser

Richard Brodhead is the president of Duke University. At the time of writing, James Moeser was the chancellor of the University of North Carolina at Chapel Hill; he is now a professor of music there.

[In April 2007] a gunman took the lives of 32 students and faculty at Virginia Tech [university in Blacksburg, Virginia]. Our nation looked on in horror, and those of us who lead universities prayed that such senseless killings would not strike our campuses again.

But they did. In February [2008], five members of the Northern Illinois University community died at the hands of a gunman.

Violence also came to our own campuses in North Carolina, with the senseless murders of Duke [University]'s Abhijit Mahato and Carolina [University]'s Eve Carson. Their deaths touched our communities deeply, just as fatal shootings had earlier at N.C. [North Carolina] Central University, UNC [University of North Carolina]-Wilmington and elsewhere in the state.

Today, as we join the rest of the country in remembering the Virginia Tech tragedy, we have learned to regard campus gun violence not as a television drama but as a life-and-death issue that directly affects universities across North Carolina. We need to do more than light candles and ring bells to remember the students we and others have lost. We must act to prevent such tragedies from recurring.

The Role of Universities

Universities have much to offer in this process, serving as a source of research, expertise and new ideas for reducing this toll. Indeed, our two campuses and others have many faculty members who could help in this process.

At Duke, for instance, Phil Cook has conducted extensive research on the costs and consequences of the widespread availability of guns. Ken Dodge is an expert on guns and gangs, and Kristin Goss' recent book examines the politics of gun control.

At UNC-Chapel Hill, Carol Runyan and others are experts on youth violence and handgun violence. Jonathan Kotch and Jon Hussey have studied the relationships between child neglect, aggression and crime. Jack Richman and social work faculty have shown how school performance and community and family concerns relate to risk factors for violence.

They and other faculty members would welcome opportunities to apply their expertise more actively on behalf of the people of North Carolina. We stand ready to help make this happen.

A common theme in all these [school violence] tragedies has been that guns were in the hands of people who shouldn't have had them.

One good place to start would be with the deep systemic problems in our criminal justice system that have been highlighted with the murders of Abhijit Mahato and Eve Carson.

Technology exists to permit law enforcement agencies and the courts to share information about criminals virtually at the press of a button. It is appalling that North Carolina has not invested in systems that would help enable judges, district attorneys, probation offices and police departments to easily share this information. Such problems must not be allowed to persist. They demand immediate action from state and local officials.

A common theme in all these tragedies has been that guns were in the hands of people who shouldn't have had them.

Hear us clearly: we are not advocating the elimination of Second Amendment [Contitution's right-to-bear-arms] rights. But we do advocate for the responsible use of and access to guns.

Getting Serious About Gun Control

Our country and state must get serious about keeping guns out of the hands or people who shouldn't have them, whether it's a troubled student at Virginia Tech or people with criminal records such as those accused in the recent murders on our two campuses. Issues of gun violence aren't simple in their solutions, but we must engage them with far greater urgency.

Over the past year, our schools have undertaken extensive efforts to strengthen their emergency response and communications systems, and to better identify and assist students who may pose a threat. In the end, however, there is only so much we can accomplish while guns remain so easily accessible.

We have had far too many anguished conversations with students who seek to understand why a bright and promising classmate has been shot dead, and with parents who worry whether their own children are safe. The best way to honor the memories of the students we have lost is to change this situation. This is why we pledge to focus our faculty expertise on these challenges and, more important, to engage with others in our communities to work together for a solution.

It is also why we believe that we, as a country, need to embrace common-sense laws about guns. This is not about politics. This is about liberals and conservatives, Republicans and

Democrats, joining together in a reasoned and dispassionate conversation about gun violence on our campuses and across America.

Gun Bans Disarm Law-Abiding Citizens, Not Criminals

John R. Lott Jr.

John Lott is a resident scholar at the American Enterprise Institute, a conservative think tank.

As Northern Illinois University restarts classes this week, one thing is clear: Six minutes proved too long.

It took six minutes before the police were able to enter the classroom that horrible Thursday [February 14, 2008], and in that short time five people were murdered, 16 wounded. Six minutes is actually record-breaking speed for the police arriving at such an attack, but it was simply not fast enough. Still, the police were much faster than at the Virginia Tech [university] attack [April 2007]. The previous Thursday [February 7, 2008], five people were killed in the city council chambers in Kirkwood, Mo. There was even a police officer already there when the attack occurred.

Gun-Free Zones Invite Attacks

But, as happens time after time in these attacks when uniformed police are there, the killers either wait for the police to leave the area or [the police] are the first people killed. In Kirkwood, the police officer was killed immediately when the attack started. People cowered or were reduced to futilely throwing chairs at the killer.

Just like attacks [in 2007] at the Westroads Mall in Omaha, Neb., the Trolley Square Mall in Salt Lake City [February 2007] and the [February 2008] attack at the Tinley Park Mall in Illinois, or all the public school attacks, they had one thing in common: They took place in "gun-free zones," where private citizens were not allowed to carry their guns with them. The malls in Omaha and Salt Lake City were in states that let people carry concealed handguns, but private property owners are allowed to post signs that ban guns; those malls were among the few places in their states that chose such a ban.

In the Trolley Square attack, an off-duty police officer fortunately violated the ban and stopped the attack. The attack at Virginia Tech or the other public school attacks occur[red] in some of the few areas within their states that people are not allowed to carry concealed handguns.

It is not just recent killings that are occurring in these gun-free zones. The Columbine High School [Littleton, Colorado] shooting left 13 murdered in 1999; Luby's Cafeteria in Killeen, Texas, had 23 who were fatally shot by a deranged man in 1991; and a McDonald's in Southern California had 21 people shot dead in 1984.

If a killer were stalking your family, would you feel safer putting a sign out front announcing, "This home is a gun-free zone"?

Nor are these horrible incidents limited to just gun-free zones in the U.S. In 1996, Martin Bryant killed 35 people in Port Arthur, Australia. In the last half-dozen years, European countries—including France, Germany and Switzerland—have experienced multiple-victim shootings. The worst in Germany resulted in 17 deaths; in Switzerland, one attack claimed the lives of 14 regional legislators.

Guns Deter Criminals

At some point you would think the media would notice that something is going on here, that these murderers aren't just picking their targets at random. And this pattern isn't really too surprising. Most people understand that guns deter criminals. If a killer were stalking your family, would you feel safer putting a sign out front announcing, "This home is a gun-free zone"? But that is what all these places did.

Even when attacks occur, having civilians with permitted concealed handguns limits the damage. A major factor in determining how many people are harmed by these killers is the amount of time that elapses between when the attack starts and someone is able to arrive on the scene with a gun.

In cases from the Colorado Springs church shooting [December 2007], in which a parishioner who was given permission by the minister to carry her concealed gun into the church quickly stopped the murder, to an attack [in 2007] in downtown Memphis to the Appalachian Law School to high schools in such places as Pearl, Miss., concealed handgun permit holders have stopped attacks well before uniformed police could possibly have arrived. [In 2008] Israeli teachers stopped a terrorist attack at a school in their country.

A number of universities . . . let students carry concealed handguns on school property.

Indeed, despite the fears being discussed about the risks of concealed handgun permit holders, I haven't found one of these multiple-victim public shootings where a permit holder has accidentally shot a bystander. With about 5 million Americans currently with concealed handgun permits in the U.S., and with states starting to have right-to-carry laws for as long as 80 years, we have a lot of experience with these laws and one thing is very clear: Concealed handgun permit holders are extremely law-abiding. Those who lose their permits for any gun-related violation are measured in the hundredths or thousandths of a percentage point.

Arming Teachers and Students

We also have a lot of experience with permitted concealed handguns in schools. Prior to the 1995 Safe School Zone Act, states with right-to-carry laws let teachers or others carry concealed handguns at school. There is not a single instance that I or others have found where this produced a single problem.

Though in a minority, a number of universities—from large public schools such as Colorado State and the University of Utah to small private schools such as Hamline in Minnesota—let students carry concealed handguns on school property. Many more schools, from Dartmouth College to Boise State University, let professors carry concealed handguns. Again, with no evidence of problems.

Few know that Dylan Klebold, one of the two Columbine killers, was closely following Colorado legislation that would have let citizens carry a concealed handgun. Klebold strongly opposed the legislation and openly talked about it. No wonder, as the bill being debated would have allowed permitted guns to be carried on school property. It is quite a coincidence that he attacked Columbine High School the very day the legislature was scheduled to vote on the bill.

With all the media coverage of the types of guns used and how the criminal obtained the gun, at some point the news media might begin to mention the one common feature of these attacks: They keep occurring in gun-free zones. Gun-free zones are a magnet for these attacks.

Gun Control Laws Have Not Reduced Violent Crime

John Stossel

John Stossel is co-anchor of the ABC News *television show* 20/20 *and the author of the book* Myth, Lies, and Downright Stupidity.

Guns are dangerous. But myths are dangerous, too. Myths about guns are very dangerous, because they lead to bad laws. And bad laws kill people. "Don't tell me this bill will not make a difference," said [former] President [Bill] Clinton, who signed the Brady Bill [restricting the purchase of handguns] into law.

Sorry. Even the federal government can't say it has made a difference. The Centers for Disease Control did an extensive review of various types of gun control: waiting periods, registration and licensing, and bans on certain firearms. It found that the idea that gun control laws have reduced violent crime is simply a myth.

Talking to Prisoners

I wanted to know why the laws weren't working, so I asked the experts. "I'm not going in the store to buy no gun," said one maximum-security inmate in New Jersey. "So, I could care less if they had a background check or not." "There's guns everywhere," said another inmate. "If you got money, you can get a gun."

Talking to prisoners about guns emphasizes a few key lessons. First, criminals don't obey the law. (That's why we call them "criminals.") Second, no law can repeal the law of supply and demand. If there's money to be made selling something, someone will sell it.

A study funded by the [U.S.] Department of Justice confirmed what the prisoners said. Criminals buy their guns illegally and easily. The study found that what felons fear most is not the police or the prison system, but their fellow citizens, who might be armed. One inmate told me, "When you gonna rob somebody you don't know, it makes it harder because you don't know what to expect out of them."

Guns and Self-Defense

What if it were legal in America for adults to carry concealed weapons? I put that question to gun-control advocate [New York social justice activist] Rev. Al Sharpton. His eyes opened wide, and he said, "We'd be living in a state of terror!" In fact, it was a trick question. Most states now have "right to carry" laws. And their people are not living in a state of terror. Not one of those states reported an upsurge in crime.

Why? Because guns are used more than twice as often defensively as criminally. When armed men broke into Susan Gonzalez' house and shot her, she grabbed her husband's gun and started firing. "I figured if I could shoot one of them, even if we both died, someone would know who had been in my home." She killed one of the intruders. She lived. Studies on defensive use of guns find this kind of thing happens at least 700,000 times a year.

A Doomsday Provision

And there's another myth, with a special risk of its own. The myth has it that the Supreme Court, in a [1939] case called *United States v. Miller*, interpreted the [U.S. Constitution's] Second Amendment—"A well regulated Militia, being necessary to the security of a free State, the right of the people to keep and bear Arms, shall not be infringed"—as conferring a special privilege on the National Guard, and not as affirming an individual right. In fact, what the court held is only that the right to bear arms doesn't mean Congress can't prohibit certain kinds of guns that aren't necessary for the common defense. Interestingly, federal law still says every able-bodied American man from 17 to 44 is a member of the United States militia.

What's the special risk? As Alex Kozinski, a federal appeals judge and an immigrant from Eastern Europe, warned in 2003, "the simple truth—born of experience—is that tyranny thrives best where government need not fear the wrath of an armed people."

"The prospect of tyranny may not grab the headlines the way vivid stories of gun crime routinely do," Judge Kozinski noted. "But few saw the Third Reich coming until it was too late. The Second Amendment is a doomsday provision, one designed for those exceptionally rare circumstances where all other rights have failed—where the government refuses to stand for reelection and silences those who protest; where courts have lost the courage to oppose, or can find no one to enforce their decrees. However improbable these contingencies may seem today, facing them unprepared is a mistake a free people get to make only once."

Gun Control Laws Will Increase Crime

Shaun Connell

Shaun Connell is a writer, blogger, public speaker, and president of the Rebirth of Freedom Foundation, a policy analysis project begun by a group of teenage conservatives and libertarians.

After heavy gun restrictions are put into place, gun crime increases. Look at the UK [United Kingdom], Australia or Washington DC for examples. The only question is—why? The answer is found through basic math and looking at the two types of gun crime statistics—the crimes caused and the crimes prevented with guns.

In 2004 the National Research Council headed a study on the impacts that gun control has on crime. The members of the research group were anti-gun and supported gun control measures. However, what they discovered was no surprise to the NRA [National Rifle Association, a gun advocacy group] and other pro-gun organizations. Gun control fails at reducing crime and suicide.

More Guns, Less Crime

The Council wrote in the research paper that,

> In summary, the committee concludes that existing research studies and data include a wealth of descriptive information on homicide, suicide, and firearms, but, because of the limitations of existing data and methods, do not credibly demonstrate a causal relationship between the ownership of firearms and the causes or prevention of criminal violence or suicide.

It's obvious by simply reading the summary that the researchers were gritting their teeth while conceding the pre-

Shaun Connell, "Gun Crime Facts," Rebirth of Freedom Foundation, December 5, 2007. Reproduced by permission.

cious yet obvious ground—but facts don't lie. The numbers are in, and gun control loses. There are several independent reasons why gun control fails, but on this page we'll be analyzing one of them: Crimes stopped mid-crime by law-abiding citizens.

Every major study dealing with gun control has discovered that the crimes stopped mid-crime by gun owners is higher than the amount of gun crimes in the United States.

The Doctors for Sensible Gun Laws is an organization dedicated to the analysis of the gun control debate. Every member of the organization is a medical doctor, PhD or holds some other form of a doctoral degree. The organization reported that,

> Research shows that guns are used much more often to prevent crimes than they are used to aid crimes. Therefore laws that hinder the ordinary citizen's right to self defense with a firearm tend to cause a net increase in crime.

What research are the Doctors for Sensible Gun Laws referring to? All of it. Literally every major study dealing with gun control has discovered that the crimes stopped mid-crime by gun owners is higher than the amount of gun crimes in the United States. This incredibly basic mathematical conflict is obvious: More Guns, Less Crime.

The most famous study on the issue is undeniably that by Gary Kleck. Criminologist Kleck, a card-carrying member of the ACLU [American Civil Liberties Union], concluded that roughly two and a half million crimes are prevented through defensive gun use alone. . . .

Simple Math

On the flip-side, guns are used in roughly 700,000 crimes. James D. Agresti explains, "In the United States during 1997, there were approximately 7,927,000 violent crimes. Of these, 691,000 were committed with firearms."

Nearly two million more crimes are prevented with guns than are "caused" by guns.

Pretending for a moment that if guns were banned that suddenly all gun crime would instantly and magically disappear, contrary to what we have learned in the UK, the question of gun control is simply a statistical tradeoff. Consider the following outrageously simply formula:

Crimes Stopped With Guns

− Guns Used by Criminals

Net Increase/Decrease of Crime

If guns stop more crimes than they cause, then "more guns, less crime." If guns cause more crimes than they stop, then "less guns, less crime." This statistical aspect of the debate is one which the anti-gun agenda conveniently ignores. And for a reason.

The above data reveals that roughly two-and-a-half million crimes are stopped with firearms. On the flipside, 700,000 crimes are committed with firearms. Using the above formula, we can conclude:

2,500,000

− 700,000

1,800,000

Nearly two million more crimes are prevented with guns than are "caused" by guns. This is the simple math—the argument that the anti-gun agenda ignores. This is also giving the agenda the benefit of the doubt—it supposes that a gun crime would have never been committed if the gun was outlawed, something that has been proven to be false in the UK.

The statistics don't lie. *Gun Crime Fact: Gun Control Kills.* More guns, less crime.

Gun Control Measures Will Not Make Our Schools Safe

Roger D. McGrath

Roger D. McGrath is a retired history professor and the author of the book Gunfighters, Highwaymen, and Vigilantes.

At about the same time [student] Cho Seung-Hui was shooting to death 32 unarmed students on the campus of Virginia Tech in Blacksburg, Virginia [in 2007], a different scenario was unfolding near Waynesburg, Kentucky. Venus Ramey had had equipment stolen from the barn on her to-bacco farm before. When she saw her dog dash into the barn, she suspected something was amiss. Balancing on her walker, the 82-year-old woman drew her snub-nosed .38 as Curtis Parrish, a would-be thief, emerged. The revolver had a salu-tary effect on Parrish, who suddenly announced that he was leaving immediately. He intended to jump into a waiting car with three of his accomplices, but Ramey yelled, "Oh, no you won't," and opened fire, flattening the car's tires. "I didn't even think twice," she later said. "If they'd even dared come close to me, they'd be six feet under by now." While Ramey held the men at gunpoint, she flagged down a passing motorist, who then called 911. Sheriff's deputies eventually took the men into custody.

Daily Occurrence

Guns are used daily by private citizens like Ramey to thwart crime and apprehend criminals. Much of the time simply brandishing a firearm is enough to do the job. Even low esti-mates of such actions state that they occur tens of thousands

Roger D. McGrath, "Making Our Schools Safe: The Virginia Tech Shooting Rampage Highlights the Vulnerability of Our Schools to Gun Violence, But the Answer to the Problem Is Not More Gun-Control," *The New American*, May 26, 2007, Vol. 23, No. 11, p. 12. Copyright © 2007 American Opinion Publishing Incorporated. Reproduced by permission.

of times a year. Gary Kleck, a Florida State University criminologist, argues that the figure is upwards of two million a year. Although guns are clearly used effectively by peaceable, law-abiding citizens far in excess of criminal misuse, such stories rarely make the news. Stories like Ramey's do nothing to further the disarmament agenda of the mainstream media.

Ramey's adventure was too juicy to ignore, however. Not only is she an octogenarian but she was Miss America 1944. She was the first redhead to win the title and a photo of her became nose art on a B-17 Flying Fortress that flew 68 missions over Germany without losing a single man. She helped sell war bonds on tours until the end of the war and then was offered a movie contract by Warner Brothers. Disgusted by Hollywood, she returned home to her Kentucky farm, married, and had two sons. She later ran for the Kentucky House of Representatives—the first Miss America to run for public office—hosted a radio show, and published a political newsletter. During, the 1970s she was instrumental in preserving a Cincinnati neighborhood, "Over-the-Rhine," and getting it listed on the National Registry of Historic Places. She made news again when she sharply criticized Vanessa Williams, Miss America 1984, for posing nude for a magazine photo spread, and Kate Shindle, Miss America 1998, who advocated condom distribution in schools. Without such a public life, Venus Ramey may have been just another of the thousands of unnoted American citizens who use firearms to defend their persons or property.

Defending Against Mass Killers

I think about this while reading analysis after analysis of Korean immigrant Cho Seung-Hui. Was he alienated, autistic, sexually frustrated, drug addled, insane? Did he play too many video games, watch too much television, view too many violent movies? This all seems less than relevant. There are a million and one reasons for criminal behavior. We, as a society, can't fix them all—although there are some that we might wish to work on. However, given the right arms and training, we can defend against such acts.

Instructive is what occurred in 2002 at another Virginia college. At Appalachian Law School in Grundy, Nigerian immigrant Peter Odighizuwa began a rampage, shooting to death a dean, a professor, and a student, and wounding three students. Upon hearing the gunfire, law students Tracy Bridges and Mikael Gross, independently, dashed to their cars to retrieve their own handguns. Bridges returned with a .357 magnum and Gross a 9 millimeter to find Odighizuwa exiting from a campus building. From different angles both Bridges and Gross leveled their weapons at Odighizuwa. Bridges yelled to the killer, "Drop your gun!" Odighizuwa did so and several students then pinned him to the ground. End of rampage.

Odighizuwa's shooting spree was widely reported. It was also widely reported that he was subdued by Appalachian students. What went mostly unreported, however, was the fact that gun-toting students were responsible for Odighizuwa having a sudden change of attitude. John Lott, Jr., a well-published researcher and writer on gun issues, said that in a Lexis-Nexis [Internet news database] search he found that only four of 208 stories mentioned that Bridges and Gross had guns. Other researchers had similar results. On the other hand, many of the stories did mention that Odighizuwa was distraught over failing grades and faced cultural differences. Psychoanalysis of the perpetrator was evidently more important than a clear narrative of events. Those interested in the former will have plenty of time to study Odighizuwa. To avoid the death penalty, he pleaded guilty to murder and is doing a life term in prison.

In Edinboro, Pennsylvania, 14-year-old Andrew Wurst came to a Parker Middle School graduation dance being held on the patio of a restaurant with a .25-caliber semiautomatic handgun. "We were all dancing and having a great time, and we heard a bang and everybody thought it was a balloon or firecracker," said a student. Science teacher John Gillette dropped to the ground dead with a bullet in his head. Wurst fired three more times, wounding another teacher and two students before the owner of the restaurant, James Strand, armed with a shotgun, put him to flight. Strand chased Wurst into a nearby field and convinced him to drop his gun and surrender. Wurst pleaded guilty to third-degree murder and was sentenced to 30–60 years in prison.

In 1997, 16-year-old Luke Woodham beat and stabbed to death his 50-year-old mother, then grabbed a .30-30 lever-action rifle and headed to his high school in Pearl, Mississippi. He shot to death his ex-girlfriend and a friend of hers and wounded seven other students. Upon hearing the first shots, Joel Myrick, the vice principal of Pearl High, ran to his pickup truck to get his .45. He had a concealed gun permit but was prohibited by law from carrying the gun onto school property. By the time Myrick caught up with Woodham, the student was hopping into his car with the intention of driving to nearby Pearl Junior High and continuing the shooting spree. Woodham started to pull away but suddenly saw Myrick aiming his gun. Unnerved, Woodham crashed the car. "Here was this monster killing kids in my school," said Myrick, "and the minute I put a gun to his head he was a kid again."

[The shooter at Virginia Tech] had no expectation that a fellow student or a faculty member might shoot back [because] Virginia Tech is a gun-free zone.

Woodham pleaded not guilty by reason of insanity and went to trial. The jury rejected his defense and found him guilty of murder. Woodham was sentenced to life in prison. One would assume that Myrick was universally hailed as a hero. Not so. During the summer of 1999, he took graduate courses in education at Harvard University. "Once people found out my story," said Myrick, "I got a lot of dirty looks and strange stares. A few people confronted me." He was treated very differently by *Soldier of Fortune* magazine. At the urging of Wayne Laugesen, a Colorado journalist and friend of Bob Brown, the publisher of *Soldier of Fortune*, the magazine awarded Myrick its Humanitarian Award of 1999 during its annual convention in Las Vegas in October [1999].

The Problem with Gun-Free Zones

If Tracy Bridges, Mikael Gross, and Joel Myrick had been carrying their guns, instead of having to sprint to their cars in distant parking lots, more students might be alive today. By contrast, restaurant owner James Strand's rapid response may have saved several lives. The attempt to make school campuses "gun-free zones" has clearly backfired. Nowhere is that more evident than at Virginia Tech. In 2006, state legislators in Virginia considered a bill that would have allowed students and professors with concealed-carry permits to bring their guns onto college campuses. When the bill died in committee, Virginia Tech associate vice president Larry Hincker declared, "I'm sure the university community is appreciative of the General Assembly's actions because this will help parents, students, faculty and visitors feel safe on our campus." He later wrote in an editorial for the [Virginia newspaper] *Roanoke Times*, "Guns don't belong in classrooms. They never will. Virginia Tech has a very sound policy preventing same."

Cho Seung-Hui brought two guns onto the campus of Virginia Tech. He shot, reloaded, shot, walked from room to room, shot, reloaded. He was in no hurry. He had no expectation that a fellow student or a faculty member might shoot back. Virginia Tech is a gun-free zone. If only a Tracy Bridges had been there with his .357 magnum.

Entire towns have declared themselves gun-free zones. In 1981, Morton Grove, Illinois, adopted a handgun ban for everyone other than police officers. Since the ban went into effect crime has increased nearly 16 percent. In 1982, Kennesaw, Georgia, took an opposite tack and passed an ordinance requiring every head of household to own and maintain a gun. Kennesaw has seen its crime rate cut in half. There are many factors at work in both towns and there is room for debate, but if the results were reversed there would be hundreds of stories screaming for gun prohibition.

The illogic of the disarmament lobby has astounded me all my life. How does disarming peaceable, law-abiding citizens make us safer? Isn't just the opposite the case? For several decades now, I have said that every "gun control" law should be titled a "Criminal Empowerment Act." With such laws criminals instantly become the one-eyed man in the valley of the blind. How can anyone believe that someone who is willing to mug, murder, or rape will be bothered by a gun law? The very notion is farcical. The illogic must originate in some deep terror of violence and the belief that laws can provide perfect safety and security, as if evil can be legislated away. Reality demonstrates that it is all well and good that sheep pass laws requiring vegetarianism, but until the wolves circling the flock agree, those laws don't mean a thing.

There is another problem, with far more dire consequences, with the disarmament lobby's illogic. In many a debate, including with representatives of the ACLU [American Civil Liberties Union], I've asked, "if, theoretically, all guns were confiscated from private citizens, criminal and law-abiding alike, who would be left with guns?" The answer, of course, is the police and the armed forces. Suddenly, the ACLU types, who are rightfully concerned about the dangers of the policing power of government and infringements on the 1st and 4th Amendments [constitutional guarantees of various freedoms, such as religion, and from unlawful search and seizure] in particular, are willing to have the same people who are otherwise their enemies—the big, bad cops and the warmongering military—own all the firepower. It seems the greatest of ironies to me.

The Wisdom of the Founding Fathers

Again, all I can conclude is that such people are so consumed with fear for their physical safety that they psychologically require an omnipotent nanny state to comfort them. And therein lies the greatest danger of all. When the people are deprived of arms and governments turn criminal, then the death toll is not in the dozens but in the thousands or millions. Just ask the Irish and Highland Scots, the Armenians, the Ukrainians, the Jews, the Chinese, the Cambodians.

Current
CONTROVERSIES

CHAPTER 3

Is Gun Control Constitutional?

Chapter Overview

Mark Tushnet

Mark Tushnet is a professor of law at Harvard Law School in Cambridge, Massachusetts.

On March 18, 2008, the U.S. Supreme Court heard oral arguments in *District of Columbia v. Heller,* a case challenging handgun-control statutes adopted in 1976 in Washington, D.C. The question before the Court is whether the District's prohibition of further registration of handguns, its ban on the carrying of concealed guns, and its mandate that guns kept in homes remain unloaded and either locked or disassembled violate citizens' rights that are guaranteed by the Second Amendment of the Constitution.[1]

Tensions Between Public Policy and the Constitution

What we do about handguns is of course a question of public policy. Because of the Second Amendment, it is also a question of constitutional law. And the point of constitutional law is to make it difficult for us to adopt some policies that seem to us to be good ones at the moment. The Supreme Court's upcoming decision in *District of Columbia v. Heller* dramatizes the tension between public policy and the Constitution.

The Second Amendment says that "a well regulated Militia, being necessary to the security of a free State, the right of the people to keep and bear Arms, shall not be infringed." Partisans on both sides think that the Amendment's meaning is

1. On June 26, 2008, the Supreme Court found in *District of Columbia v. Heller* that the Second Amendment protects an individual's right to possess a firearm for private use.

Mark Tushnet, "Interpreting the Right to Bear Arms—Gun Regulation and Constitutional Law," *The New England Journal of Medicine*, April 3, 2008, Vol. 358, No. 14, p. 1424.

clear. According to gun-control advocates, the opening reference to a militia means that the right protected in the second clause is necessarily limited to keeping and bearing arms in connection with service in an organized militia. According to gun-rights advocates, the second part of the Amendment protects an individual right, no different in kind from the right of free speech protected by the First Amendment.

In fact, interpreting the Second Amendment is a genuinely difficult task, precisely because we have to determine the relation between the first clause, sometimes called the Amendment's preamble, and the second, sometimes called its operative clause. The preamble could be a condition, limiting the scope of the operative clause, or it could merely be an explanation: "The reason people have an individual right to keep and bear arms is that it makes it easier to provide a militia as the security to a free state."(In the case of *District of Columbia v. Heller,* there's some basically silly discussion of whether the Second Amendment even applies to the District, since it isn't a "state." It's quite clear that the term in the Second Amendment refers to organized governments and not to the narrower group of subnational units we call the states of the United States.) . . .

Gun-control advocates point out that when the term "militia" is used elsewhere in the Constitution, it always refers to the state-organized militia (roughly, though imperfectly, analogous to today's state-organized National Guard). So, they argue, the Second Amendment's preamble also refers to the state-organized militia. To them, the Amendment is part of a package of constitutional provisions expressing the framers' suspicion of a permanent national army. It guarantees that Congress cannot disarm the state-organized militia. They also point out that in the late 18th century, individuals might have been considered to have a right to "keep" arms, but the phrase "keep and bear arms" was used only in reference to military operations.

Gun-rights advocates have a different view. Their strongest point is that the Bill of Rights is a bill of individual rights. They argue that the Second Amendment's preamble explains why we have an individual right to keep and bear arms. And the "militia" mentioned in the preamble, in this view, is not the state-organized militia but rather what 18th-century thinkers described as the unorganized militia, the whole body of the people who, if armed, would be able to resist efforts by an oppressive government or to provide self-protection when the government failed in its duty to protect against predators and criminals.

This reading does make sense of the preamble's reference to the militia—but at some cost. If the point of the Second Amendment is to allow the body of the people to resist an oppressive government, isn't the Amendment entirely obsolete? Modern governments have tanks and bombs that they could use against the people, and surely, as gun-control advocates say, we can't fairly interpret the Second Amendment as guaranteeing the people a right to own antitank weapons and bazookas. Interpreting the Amendment as protecting weapon ownership only in connection with membership in a state-organized militia avoids this difficulty.

Legal Tradition

Such are the arguments regarding the Second Amendment's language as it might have been understood when it was adopted. But constitutional interpretation also takes into account relevant legal tradition; unfortunately, both sides have good arguments on this front as well. On the gun-control side, there's the undoubted fact that state governments have regulated weapon ownership quite extensively since early in the 19th century. The national government didn't get involved in large-scale weapon regulation until the 20th century. But when it did, the courts routinely upheld the regulation because they believed that the Second Amendment protected a right only in connection with membership in a state-organized militia. (see Key Court Rulings about Gun Regulation and the Second Amendment). Such a tradition of extensive regulation of gun ownership that was upheld against constitutional challenge should count for something.

Gun-rights advocates point to another tradition: many state constitutions provide guarantees of what is clearly an individual right to own weapons. And the Supreme Court has said—in cases involving the death penalty and assisted suicide—that state-level traditions properly influence the interpretation of provisions in the national Constitution.

The briefs filed in the D.C. case make many additional arguments, but the constitutional question is genuinely difficult. (For what it's worth, my own view is that the gun-rights side has a slightly better argument than its opponents if we focus only on the time when the Amendment was adopted and that the gun-control side has a slightly better argument than its opponents if we use the whole range of constitutional arguments that the courts have said usually matter. But for me, both debates are too close to call.)

The Task Before the Supreme Court

So what can we expect from the Supreme Court? Early in the [George W.] Bush administration, the Department of Justice issued an extensive legal analysis supporting the gun-rights view of the Second Amendment. It has adhered to that position in the D.C. case but with an important twist. Suppose the Second Amendment does protect an individual right. Still, like all rights, that right can be regulated by the government for good reasons—as the Amendment's reference to a "well regulated" militia itself suggests. In the First Amendment setting, we let the government regulate speech only if it has extremely good reasons for the regulation.

The Bush administration argues in the D.C. case that what lawyers call the "standard of review" for gun regulations is different from that for speech regulations. Lawyers delineate three categories of reasons for regulation: In instances in which really good reasons should be required for restricting a specific right, the regulations are subject to "strict scrutiny" by the courts; in situations in which relatively strong but not overwhelming reasons should be required, the regulations are subject to "intermediate scrutiny"; and when legislators just ought to have some modest reason for thinking that the regulation does some good, the regulation is subject only to "rational basis review." The Bush administration says that the District's handgun ban is subject to intermediate scrutiny and that there is some reason to think it could survive such scrutiny.

The first question the Supreme Court will have to confront in the D.C. case is whether the Second Amendment does indeed protect an individual right. If it finds that it does, the Court will have to decide what standard of review to apply to gun regulations. That, I suspect, is where the real action will be. Nonlawyers watching the Court's decision should focus on the bottom line. If the Court affirms the lower court, it will have held that the Second Amendment protects an individual right and that the District's handgun ban cannot survive the appropriate level of scrutiny. If it vacates the lower court's decision, the Court will be saying that the handgun ban might be constitutional if the lower courts apply the correct standard of review. And if it reverses the lower court, the Court will have rejected the "individual rights" interpretation of the Second Amendment altogether.

Guns Are No Longer Needed to Protect Democracy

Nasir Ahmed

Nasir Ahmed is a professor of political science at Grambling State University, a college in Grambling, Louisiana.

Gun violence is taking too many lives in America. Liberal gun laws and the Second Amendment right to own [a] gun has made America a very dangerous society to live in. Gun violence is disproportionately affecting the African-Americans and the people at the low socio-economic level.

Gun Violence in America

The debate around the Second Amendment is mindboggling; politics almost always takes over common sense. Studies have found the United States has by far the highest rate of gun deaths—murders, suicides, and accidents—among the world's richest nations. Japan had the lowest rate. In 2004, there were 29,569 gun-related deaths in the United States, including almost 12,000 homicides, more than 16,750 suicides and approximately 650 unintentional deaths. Every day, more than 80 Americans die from gun violence—almost 2.5 times of the number of persons killed at Virginia Tech [referring to the 2007 mass murder at the university] each day.

The rate of firearm deaths among kids under age 15 is almost 12 times higher in the United States than in 25 other industrialized countries combined. American kids are 16 times more likely to be murdered with a gun, 11 times more likely to commit suicide with a gun, and nine times more likely to die from a firearm accident than children in 25 other industrialized countries combined.

Nasir Ahmed, "Gun Violence and Revisiting the Second Amendment," *The Gramblinite*, May 1, 2008. Reproduced by permission.

There were also approximately 70,000 non-fatal gun shot injuries in 2005 serious enough to require at least an emergency room visit. In addition, there were 477,040 victims of gun-related crimes in the United States in 2005. In a single year, 3,012 children and teens were killed by gunfire in the United States, according to the data released in 2002.

That is one child every three hours; eight children every day; and more than 50 children every week. And every year, at least 4 to 5 times as many kids and teens suffer from non-fatal firearm injuries. America is losing too many children to gun violence. Between 1979 and 2001, gunfire killed 90,000 children and teens in America and in one year, more children and teens died from gunfire than from cancer, pneumonia, influenza, asthma, and HIV/AIDS combined.

Freedom No Longer Linked to Guns

We live in a society where access to [a] gun is clearly responsible for so many deaths. So it makes sense to restrict that access. The Second Amendment was designed to protect individual rights in a manner that was consistent with the need of that time. Democracy was not institutionalized and our freedom was in danger from the British Empire in [the] late 18th century.

Having access to guns is not making America more or less democratic or for that matter more or less free.

Freedom was linked with people having access to guns. At the dawn of the 21st century that paradigm does not exist. We don't have to worry [about] another country making us a colony nor do we have to worry about America becoming [an] autocratic nation.

Even if the Federal Government becomes an autocratic nation, we have to fight that struggle in a different way; our guns can't match our mighty federal power. We have to keep in mind, our constitution is institutionalized—and so is our democracy and freedom.

Having access to guns is not making America more or less democratic or for that matter more or less free. Linking gun[s] with freedom and democracy is rather silly; it reflects one's lack of understanding of the world we live in, particularly in a seasoned and matured democracy like the USA.

Studies have found strong correlation between access to guns and violence again and again. Households with guns are more likely to experience violence, suicide and death by using guns.

The Second Amendment Is Misused by Opponents of Gun Control

Saul Cornell

Saul Cornell is a professor of history at Ohio State University and author of the book A Well Regulated Militia: The Founding Fathers and the Origins of Gun Control in America.

Few issues in America are more controversial than guns. Yet even among hot button topics in American public life there is something perverse about the dynamics of the debate over guns.

Polling data for decades have shown that most Americans favor stronger gun laws. Indeed, surveys demonstrate that such policies are even supported by most gun owners. Yet pundits and political soothsayers have written off this issue because it is perceived to be a loser at the polls.

The Relationship Between Gun Rights and Gun Control

Gun rights and gun control have long histories. Although both sides in the great American gun debate have claimed to have history on their side, each has presented a version of the past that is highly selective. One of the many embarrassing truths about the debate over the right to bear arms that neither side wishes to admit is that gun rights ideology is the illegitimate and spurned child of gun control.

Efforts at gun control, particularly policies aimed at broad scale prohibitions of firearms, have generally led to an intensification of gun rights rhetoric and activism. Understanding the history of this tangled relationship, one of American

Saul Cornell, "It's Time for Gun Control Proponents to Reclaim the Constitutional High Ground," *History News Network*, May 15, 2006. Reproduced by permission.

history's more bizarre examples of ideological co-dependency, may provide some insights into how we might move this debate forward and break this cycle.

As long as there have been guns in America there have been regulations governing their use and storage. Without government direction there would have been no body of Minutemen [early American militia volunteers] to muster on the town greens at Lexington and Concord. If the Founders had imbibed the strong gun rights ideology that drives today's gun debate we would all be drinking tea and singing, "God save our gracious Queen."

The Right to Be Free from Gun Violence

Ironically, the Second Amendment [of the Constitution, guaranteeing the right to bear arms] does not prohibit robust gun regulation, it compels it. Today's gun rights ideology is antithetical to the original understanding of the Second Amendment and only emerged in the 19th century when individual states began passing the first gun control laws to deal with the new problems posed by hand guns.

The right to be free from the threat of gun violence deserves as much respect as the right to bear arms.

[New York City] Mayor Michael Bloomberg's recent summit on gun violence reminds us that this is not the first time in American history that gun violence and gun control have been on the minds of New Yorkers. DeWitt Clinton, mayor from 1803 to 1815, bemoaned the problem posed by hand guns almost two hundred years ago.

There is much to be learned from America's first gun violence crisis and the first gun control movement. It is not surprising that during that struggle gun rights supporters tried to lay claim to the Second Amendment by reinterpreting it as an individual right of self defense. This argument continues to be effectively employed by opponents of gun regulation.

Modern gun control proponents have generally been embarrassed by the Second Amendment, viewing it as an anachronism. Early proponents of gun regulation did not make the same mistake. Rather than dismiss the Second Amendment as a remnant of America's revolutionary past, they venerated it, reminding their opponents that the Second Amendment was about an obligation citizens owed to their government and communities to contribute to public defense. They also staked out another right that has not been much talked about recently in this debate: a right to be free from the fear of gun violence.

What does all of this mean for the contemporary gun debate? Proponents of gun control must not demonize gun owners, particularly given the fact that most gun owners support reasonable gun regulation. Any solution to America's gun problem must have the support of gun owners.

Rather than abandon the Second Amendment and dismiss it as a relic of another era, supporters of gun regulation need to reclaim this part of our constitutional heritage. Supporters of regulation need to point out that liberty without regulation is impossible. The right to be free from the threat of gun violence deserves as much respect as the right to bear arms.

The U.S. Supreme Court Should Uphold the District of Columbia's Handgun Ban

Matthew Cooper

Matthew Cooper is a Washington, D.C., journalist and former reporter for Time *magazine.*

On the night of November 17 [2007], I was at a bar mitzvah for the son of an officer of a top investment bank. It was a wonderful, lavish affair held for about 200 guests at a synagogue in Washington [D.C.]'s affluent Cleveland Park neighborhood. There was a video tribute to the boy and a seated dinner served under pasha-style tents.

Across town that evening, another young man, Tim Spicer, was getting off work at Ben's Chili Bowl in the U Street corridor, a neighborhood once known as the black Broadway because the likes of [mid-twentieth-century jazz musician] Duke Ellington performed there. I had become friends with Tim after years of eating at Ben's, a D.C. institution whose walls are adorned with photos of such famous customers as Bono and Bill Cosby. He was fantastically nice. He always helped me jump the line to get a half-smoke, my regular artery-clogging sausage. He would chat with my nine-year-old son and tell me about his aspirations. Tim had dropped out of high school, but he got his G.E.D. [high school diploma equivalent] and wanted to attend Howard University. In his spare time, he rapped and drew fashion sketches. He hoped to start a clothing line, and we had talked about my investing in it.

As I was eating sushi at the synagogue, Tim was murdered. According to the police department's reconstruction of events, he was carjacked. The killer (or killers) drove away in Tim's souped-up 1994 Chevy Caprice and Tim stumbled to a nearby Metro stop, where he died. He was 25 and a father.

The [Supreme] court has assiduously avoided ruling on gun control since the 1930s . . . [but] it's deciding a case that could strike down many of the country's gun laws.

Ten days later, I went to his funeral. Mourners wailed at his open casket. Speaker after speaker praised his kindness and asked God what was happening to so many young black men. Tim's murder was the 169th in D.C. in 2007, which gave it notoriety. The previous year, there had been 169 murders in the District, so each one after Tim's underscored the city's rising homicide rate. Police have yet to make an arrest or disclose the weapon that killed Tim, but odds are it was a handgun, the weapon of choice in American cities.

The *Heller* Case

A few days after Tim was slain, the U.S. Supreme Court accepted *District of Columbia v. Heller*, a case about a law that was supposed to prevent murders like Tim's: D.C.'s ban on handguns, the country's strictest gun-control measure. Constitutional scholars, gun manufacturers, and gun-control advocates say this will be the most significant firearms case to come before the high court in almost 70 years. The court has assiduously avoided ruling on gun control since the 1930s, when it opened the door to regulation; suddenly it's deciding a case that could strike down many of the country's gun laws affecting every firearm owner and manufacturer.[1] How this case got to the [Chief Justice John] Roberts court, and its coming as I dealt for the first time with a friend becoming a murder victim, made me ponder the prevalence of gun vio-

1. On June 26, 2008, the Supreme Court found in *District of Columbia v. Heller* that the Second Amendment protects an individual's right to possess a firearm for private use.

lence, the complexity of the issue's policy and politics, and why both sides, I think, miss the point.

It's easy for liberals to view the gun lobby as monolithic. In left-wing demonology, the National Rifle Association [N.R.A.] is regarded, along with Halliburton [multinational corporation accused of war profiteering], as all-powerful. But the gun movement is more nuanced than that. In 2000, for instance. Smith & Wesson, the nation's largest gun manufacturer, broke with the rest of the gun industry and signed a settlement agreement with the Clinton administration in order to avoid lawsuits. The company, more than 150 years old, agreed to adopt numerous safety measures and change its sales practices. Smith & Wesson found itself vilified, subject to boycotts by weapons enthusiasts who believed it had sold out.

Indeed, *District of Columbia v. Heller* actually reached the court over the N.R.A.'s objections. Alan Gura, one of the lawyers challenging the ban, told me that the N.R.A. originally opposed bringing the case, fearing it could lead to a ruling that would establish a government right to regulate arms sales. The N.R.A. believes that its famously effective lobbying finds a more receptive forum in Congress and state legislatures than in the less predictable courts. Gun manufacturers—closely aligned with the N.R.A., especially since the Smith & Wesson boycott—also would rather have skipped the courts.

While the case has some surprising opponents, its advocates defy stereotyping too. Robert Levy, a scholar at the Cato Institute, a libertarian think tank, doesn't own a gun and doesn't want to. Still, as a libertarian, Levy had long nursed the idea of filing a lawsuit that would resolve the gun-control debate on the side of individuals who want to buy guns. Using the fortune he made in the securities industry, Levy financed the case, and rather than recruiting cliché gun nuts for plaintiffs, he enlisted a diverse group to bring the suit. One of them is a middle-aged gay man who bought a gun to defend himself from attacks by bigots.

Let the People Decide

District of Columbia v. Heller revolves around the question of whether D.C.'s gun ban is unconstitutional, a violation of the right to bear arms guaranteed by the Second Amendment. The court could make a sweeping ruling about whether the Constitution allows individual gun ownership to be regulated at all. Last March [2007], the U.S. Court of Appeals for the D.C. Circuit considered to be the nation's second-highest court, ruled that the D.C. law was unconstitutional because the right to bear arms applies to all individuals, not just those in a militia, as the Second Amendment suggests.

No one knows what will happen with the case in the Roberts court, but I know what I would do. I have no personal interest in guns, and I'm agnostic as to whether gun bans really do anything to prevent crimes like the one that ended Tim's life. Obviously, the law in D.C. did not save Tim: it seems to have served only to disarm the law-abiding. I believe the District's ban is draconian [unnecessarily severe]: It holds that just current and retired police officers can own handguns. You can own a rifle but it must be disassembled, making it impossible to use for self-defense. It seems crazy that the named litigant in the case, Dick Heller, who carries a handgun for his job as a guard at a courthouse, can't have one in his home because security guards are technically not police officers. It's one thing to regulate gun sales, but a flat-out ban seems like bad policy in terms of its effectiveness and whom it affects.

Still, I hope the court upholds the ban. It's overwhelmingly popular here; no D.C. council member wants it repealed. I'm not a lawyer, let alone a scholar, but I see no reason to interpret the Second Amendment as forbidding a jurisdiction from banning a particular weapon, whether it's an assault rifle or a handgun. As Linda Singer, D.C.'s former attorney general, told me, "Banning one particularly dangerous arm does not mean banning the right to bear arms." She notes that handguns are by far the predominant weapon used in murders and suicides in Washington [D.C.] and elsewhere. In 1976, the District's second year of autonomous home rule, the gun ban was one of the first laws passed, in part because all of the city's rapes in 1974 that involved a firearm were committed with a handgun.

In the wake of Tim's murder, it would be easy to give a knee-jerk liberal or conservative response: We need more gun control; we need less gun control. But the most important thing, to me anyway, is who decides. That ought to be the people of D.C., like Tim's grieving family, through their elected representatives. Tim's life is too precious to be reduced to either side's talking point.

The U.S. Supreme Court Should Rule That the Right to Bear Arms Is Subject to Reasonable Regulation

Allen Rostron

Allen Rostron is on the faculty of the University of Missouri-Kansas City School of Law and a former senior staff attorney for the Brady Center to Prevent Gun Violence.

In a few months, the U.S. Supreme Court will issue the most important decision it has ever made about the Second Amendment. Who will win? If the Court wisely heads for the sensible middle ground, everybody will win.

Key Questions in the *Heller* Case

The last time the Court made a significant pronouncement about the meaning of the right "to keep and bear arms" was in *United States v. Miller* (1939), a cryptic opinion which raised more questions than it answered. After avoiding the issue for nearly seventy years, the Court is finally poised to shed new light on the Second Amendment's meaning in *District of Columbia v. Heller*. That case concerns the constitutionality of D.C. laws that essentially ban handguns and require other firearms, such as rifles and shotguns, to be kept unloaded and disassembled or bound by a trigger lock or similar device while stored in gun owners' homes.

Since the Court heard oral argument in the *Heller* case on March 18 [2008], gun control supporters and opponents alike have been busy scrutinizing the justices' questions and remarks for clues to how they will rule.

Some press coverage of the case has had an unfortunate tendency to oversimplify the legal issues, suggesting that the key question is whether the Court will decide that the Second Amendment protects an "individual right" as opposed to a "state right." In fact, the District of Columbia does not deny that the Second Amendment protects a right that belongs to individuals, so that point is not even disputed in the case.

Instead, the real question that has been hotly debated for several decades is the scope or breadth of that right. Is it a right that applies only in connection with public, organized, military activity? Or is it a right that applies more broadly to self-defense and other private uses of guns?

Thousands of pages of law journals, books, and briefs have been filled with arguments about that question over the years. The result essentially has been an unsatisfying draw. There is ample material to support both sides of the debate, whether one looks at the constitutional text, the historical record surrounding its adoption, the underlying concerns that inspired the provision, or its origins in English legal history.

No Correct Answer

Reading the endless stream of writing on this question, both as a lawyer for a gun control organization and then as a law professor, convinced me that there simply is no clear "correct" answer to the question of how broadly the Second Amendment should reach. The meaning of the Amendment is in the eye of the beholder, with both sides equally and sincerely able to find what they want to see.

I am convinced that if we could go back in time and ask the Framers [of the Constitution] about the scope of the Amendment, we would hear a wide range of different views. Military use of guns was the overwhelming focus of the discussion for those who drafted and adopted the Amendment. But did they also expect it to cover other uses of guns? Surely some did, and some did not, and most probably never thought about it one way or the other. To say that we can look back now and determine what was the majority view, on an issue that was clearly not the center of attention, is to pretend that we know more than we really do.

No matter how much of a genuine toss-up the issue may be, the Supreme Court probably cannot avoid picking one side or the other. The justices' statements at the oral argument, as well as their previous comments and general ideological leanings, strongly suggest that at least five of them will endorse the view that the Second Amendment extends broadly to reach more than just military activities.

Rather than resolving the case, that will merely lead to the most crucial question of all. How strong is the right protected by the Second Amendment? In other words, what level of scrutiny or review should be applied to decide the constitutionality of the host of federal, state, and local gun laws in force today?

The Appropriate Legal Standard

The District of Columbia argues that laws should be upheld if they represent "reasonable restrictions." If the Supreme Court agrees, it will be supported by an overwhelming consensus that already exists at the state constitutional level. Adam Winkler, a professor of constitutional law at UCLA [University of California at Los Angeles], has done magnificent work showing that there has long been widespread agreement in state courts across the country on the test that should be used in gun cases. Forty-two states have constitutional provisions that give individuals a right to have guns for non-military activities. In every instance, courts have held that this right protects people from being completely disarmed, but gives governments wide room to impose reasonable regulations on guns.

Heller, and *amici* [non-parties who file briefs in a case] like the National Rifle Association, urge the Court to apply strict scrutiny [a very high level of review]. That would be an unprecedented and enormous mistake. None of the lower federal or state courts that have recognized a broad individual right to guns has concluded that strict scrutiny should apply. Strict scrutiny would lead to a crushing wave of constitutional challenges to every firearm law in the nation and risk invalidation of even the most reasonable, common sense restrictions on guns.

If the Court agrees with Heller that the Second Amendment protects a broad individual right to have guns for nonmilitary purposes, but also concludes that the right is subject to reasonable regulations, the Court will have made a decision that both sides truly could call a victory. In particular, gun owners would be reassured that they are protected by a constitutional right. They could stop being afraid that every gun regulation, no matter how modest, will lead the country down a "slippery slope" to bans and confiscations of all guns.

The most important thing the Court will do is set the legal standard that governs future challenges to gun control laws.

The ultimate fate of the statutes at issue in the *District of Columbia v. Heller* case—D.C.'s handgun ban and gun storage requirements—matter much less than the crucial question of what test or standard of scrutiny comes out of the Court's decision and applies in future cases. Indeed, if the Court really wants to emphasize that it is coming down squarely in the middle on this often polarizing subject, it could strike down one part of the D.C. law and uphold the other. Chief Justice John Roberts gave tantalizing hints during oral arguments that he might support such a compromise, suggesting several times that he could not regard a complete ban on handguns as reasonable, but also that he might be more inclined to uphold the safe storage law. The Court also could easily split the case in the opposite direction, concluding that D.C. homeowners should be allowed to store guns unlocked and ready to be used against criminals, but that banning handguns is a reasonable restriction considering that shotguns traditionally have been regarded as excellent weapons for home security.

Whatever decision the Court makes about the validity of the D.C. laws, the most important thing the Court will do is set the legal standard that governs future challenges to gun control laws. The vast majority of the American people oppose complete bans on guns, but support reasonable restrictions. By approaching the *Heller* case in a spirit of conciliation and compromise rather than extremism, the Court can make the decision a victory for everyone, affirming the validity of reasonable regulations while respecting the interests of gun owners.[1]

---

1. On June 26, 2008, the Supreme Court upheld the lower court, finding Washington's handgun ban to be unconstitutional.

Citizens Still Need Guns to Protect Themselves Against Bad Government

John F. McManus

John F. McManus is president of the John Birch Society, an extremely conservative political organization, and publisher of The New American *magazine.*

Aaron Zelman is executive director of Jews for the Preservation of Firearms Ownership [JPFO], a pro-Second Amendment group based in Milwaukee [Wisconsin].

John F. McManus of The New American*: What is your organization's main goal?*

Aaron Zelman: Our main goal is to destroy gun control. We are an organization that believes we have the moral authority to point out to the rest of the world the evils that have come from gun control and how humanity has suffered because of gun-control schemes.

Are people who aren't Jewish members of your organization?

We have members of our organization that have told us they are not Jewish. We don't ask people what their religion is. And we are not an organization that is preaching religion to anybody. We think the history of gun-control schemes has been so harmful to Jews that we have the moral authority to speak out. We welcome anybody who accepts the JPFO position that gun control must be destroyed. We're not interested in compromise. We are only interested in the destruction of something we consider to be a very evil and deadly policy known as gun control.

John F. McManus, "No Compromise Against Gun Control: Aaron Zelman Interviewed," *The New American*, May 26, 2008. Reproduced by permission.

How did you become involved in something like this?

Well, I've been involved in promoting gun ownership because of my family history to some degree. When my father was about six months old, his family had to leave the Ukraine in Russia because [Soviet Union dictator Joseph] Stalin came to power. Stalin was not interested in kulaks [Russian peasants] owning land. And so they lost everything they had, essentially, and fled to Canada where my dad was raised and served in the Canadian Army during World War II. So, I learned at a very, very early age what happens when you can't defend your life against a government gone bad.

Could you give us some examples of what has happened in other nations where gun control was in place?

Well, there are several. Why don't we start with the film we created called *Innocents Betrayed?*. The film shows the history of and the connection between gun registration, confiscation, and how a police state is able to come about. It shows how the police state can target individuals they don't want to live and murder them—otherwise known as genocide.

Where has this happened?

Historically it happened in Turkey, known as the Armenian Genocide, and then, of course, in China, Russia, Germany, Cambodia, Rwanda, Uganda, and even now in Darfur.

You've actually obtained some of the documents from these different countries, and you've translated them so that we who read only English can read them?

A number of years ago we started this project of trying to find out if there was a connection among governments and if governments did the same thing. As we put it, these folks all go to the same dictators' school. Indeed, there is a connection because there is a pattern. They realize they can't stay in power if the peasants have pitchforks and can march on the gates of the city. The way to bring about a dictatorship or police state is to make sure the people are disarmed.

I understand you have done work showing the source of the 1968 gun law here in the United States.

The 1968 Gun Control Act, as we know it today, became law during the [Lyndon B.] Johnson administration. The history behind the 1968 act is indeed fascinating. The author of the federal Gun Control Act, Senator Thomas Dodd, was an attorney with the U.S. Justice Department at Nuremberg [Germany, where he helped in the prosecution of Nazi war criminals]. He obtained the *Reichsgesetzblatt*, which is the German equivalent of our *Federal Register*. He was able to use the German gun-control laws after giving them to the Library of Congress to translate for him. They did indeed translate the laws for him, and that was the model, the basis, for the 1968 Gun Control Act in America.

Many Americans believe that it is the duty of police to protect them. Comment?

There is no duty for the police to protect an individual unless there's been a prior agreement that they will offer you protection.

The police do not have a duty to protect individuals. The shield on the side of the car may say "to protect and serve," but the reality is, and by state law and the state statutes and case law, you do not have a right to police protection.

We have a book we publish entitled *Dial 911 and Die*. It's written by an attorney named Richard Stevens. The book details laws in every single state in the Union, the state statutes as well as case law, concerning calling 911.

You can sue the police if they fail to protect you, and your heirs can sue the police if you die during a criminal's attack on you, but you won't accomplish anything because the judge will finally tell you that there is no duty for the police to protect an individual unless there's been a prior agreement that they will offer you protection. If you've been an informant for the police, if you are involved in some type of work for the police where the police are not able to protect you, if it's dangerous work, you are entitled. But short of that the police have no duty to protect you.

Could you tell us about "Goody Guns"?

Goody Guns is a program we started to save our children from the clutches of the gun prohibitionists in the public school system. Goody Guns are cookie cutters in the shape of revolvers or pistols, and the purpose of using them as you bake cookies for your children, or grandchildren, is to teach them firearm safety while they are eating their cookie.

You tell them to eat the cookie from the back of the gun where the handle is to the front of the gun where the muzzle is. And so they learn an important fact on firearms safety—controlling where the muzzle is pointed. You start early with the Goody Guns, and by the time they get to the public school system and they hear all the propaganda about guns being bad, they will know better.

Our country became independent because citizens were armed.

When we first introduced Goody Guns, gun prohibitionists had a conniption fit because they knew the psychology behind our program. They realized they can't get into your home when the kid is two years old; they have to wait until your child is six years old in the school system, and by then they've lost.

Once Goody Guns went up on the Internet, everybody knew about it. We had, concerning Goody Guns, a call from a television station in England that was producing a program on guns in America. And they were curious about Goody Guns.

The person who called me wanted to know what the rationale behind Goody Guns was, and I sensed from the way she was asking the questions that she was trying to figure out a way to maneuver something to cause us a problem. Finally, she acknowledged, after we were almost done, that this was very clever and would probably be very effective. End of conversation. She put the phone down.

Have you been blasted by the media for this?

Well, the media is being true to form. They want to ignore anything that JPFO does. But the gun prohibitionists remain incensed. They had to speak out against it.

What's the greatest threat on the horizon right now for the right to keep and bear arms?

I think there are numerous threats, but one is that the American public really doesn't understand a need for an armed citizenry. Our country became independent because citizens were armed. This is why an organized, state-controlled militia received attention in the U.S. Constitution. So we have a lot of work to do. We have to reach out to people and help them understand why citizens must be armed, and what's happened to citizens throughout the world and throughout history when they couldn't defend themselves against a government gone bad.

The Second Amendment Right to Bear Arms Is an Individual Right

Wall Street Journal

The Wall Street Journal *is an international daily newspaper specializing in finance.*

In recent decades, the Supreme Court has discovered any number of new rights not in the explicit text of the Constitution. Now it has the opportunity to validate a right that resides in plain sight—"the right of the people to keep and bear arms" in the Second Amendment.

This week [early in 2007], the Supreme Court agreed to hear the case of *District of Columbia v. Heller.* In March [2007], the Court of Appeals for the D.C. Circuit declared unconstitutional the District's near-total ban on handgun possession. That 2-1 ruling, written by Judge Laurence Silberman, found that when the Second Amendment spoke of the "right of the people," it meant the right of "individuals," and not some "collective right" held only by state governments or the National Guard.

That stirring conclusion was enough to prompt the D.C. government to declare Judge Silberman outside "the mainstream of American jurisprudence" in its petition to the Supreme Court. We've certainly come to an interesting legal place if asserting principles that appear nowhere in the Constitution is considered normal, but it's beyond the pale to interpret the words that are in the Constitution to mean what they say.

However, it is true that, despite our vitriolic policy fights over gun control, the Supreme Court has rarely ruled on the

Second Amendment. The Court last spoke in detail in 1939, in *U.S. v. Miller*, involving a bootlegger who claimed the right to transport an unregistered sawed-off shotgun across state lines. That opinion was sufficiently complicated that both sides now claim it as a precedent.

The dispute arises from the first four words of the Second Amendment, the full text of which reads: "A well regulated Militia, being necessary to the security of a free State, the right of the people to keep and bear Arms, shall not be infringed." If the first two clauses were omitted, there would be no room for ambiguity. But part of the legal controversy has centered around what a "well regulated militia" means.

Judge Silberman's opinion argued, with convincing historical evidence, that the "militia" the Framers [of the Constitution] had in mind was not the National Guard of the present, but referred to all able-bodied male citizens who might be called upon to defend their country. The notion that the average American urbanite might today go to his gun locker, grab his rifle and sidearm and rush, Minuteman-like, to his nation's defense might seem quaint. But at stake is whether the "militia" of the Second Amendment is some small, discreet group of people acting under government control, or all of us.

The phrase "the right of the people" or some variation of it appears repeatedly in the [Constitution's] Bill of Rights, and nowhere does it actually mean "the right of the government." When the Bill of Rights was written and adopted, the rights that mattered politically were of one sort—an individual's, or a minority's, right to be free from interference from the state. Today, rights are most often thought of as an entitlement to receive something *from* the state, as opposed to a freedom from interference *by* the state. The Second Amendment is, in our view, clearly a right of the latter sort.

As a practical matter on the Court, the outcome in *D.C. v. Heller* might well be decided by one man: Anthony Kennedy, the most protean of Justices. However, in recent years he has also been one of the most aggressive Justices in asserting any number of other rights to justify his opinions on various social issues. It would seriously harm the Court's credibility if Justice Kennedy and the Court's liberal wing now turned around and declared the right "to keep and bear arms" a dead letter because it didn't comport with their current policy views on gun control. This potential contradiction may explain why no less a liberal legal theorist than Harvard's Laurence Tribe has come around to an "individual rights" understanding of the Second Amendment.

By the way, a victory for gun rights in *Heller* would not ban all gun regulation, any more than the Court's support for the First Amendment bars every restraint on free speech. The Supreme Court has allowed limits on speech inciting violence or disrupting civil order. In the same way, a judgment that the Second Amendment is an individual right could allow reasonable limits on gun use, such as to protect public safety.

Here's hoping the Justices will put aside today's gun control passions and look to the plain language of the Bill of Rights for instruction in this case, as Judge Silberman had the courage to do.

The Ninth and Fourteenth Amendments Support Gun Rights

Akhil Reed Amar

Akhil Reed Amar teaches constitutional law at Yale University and is the author of the book, America's Constitution: A Biography.

The language of the Second Amendment has been the obsessive focus of just about everyone interested in *District of Columbia v. Heller*, the D.C. gun-ownership case to be [decided by] the Supreme Court.[1] . . . That amendment is indeed important and much misunderstood. But *Heller*'s facts, which involve the possession of a gun inside the home for self-defense, lie rather far from the Second Amendment's core concerns, as originally understood by the Founding Fathers. To think straight about gun control and the Constitution, we need to move past the Second Amendment and pay more heed to the Ninth and 14th Amendments.

The Ninth Amendment's Support for Gun Rights

Let's begin here: Suppose, for argument's sake, that we concede that everything gun-control advocates say about the Second Amendment is right. Suppose that the amendment focused solely on arms-bearing in military contexts, and that it said absolutely nothing about an individual's right to have a gun while sleeping in his own home or hunting in his own

---

1. On June 26, 2008, the Supreme Court found in *District of Columbia v. Heller* that the Second Amendment protects an individual's right to possess a firearm for private use.

private Idaho. Would this concession mean that no individual constitutional right exists today? Hardly. According to the Ninth Amendment: "The enumeration in the Constitution of certain rights shall not be construed to deny or disparage other rights retained by the people." In other words, there may well be constitutional rights that are not explicitly set forth in the Second Amendment (or in any other amendment or constitutional clause, for that matter).

In identifying these unenumerated "rights retained by the people," the key is that a judge should not decide what he or she personally thinks would be a proper set of rights. Instead, the judge should ask which rights have been recognized by the American people themselves—for example, in state constitutions and state bills of rights and civil rights laws. Americans have also established, merely by living our lives freely across the country and over the centuries, certain customary rights that governments have generally respected. Many of our most basic rights are simply facts of life, the residue of a virtually unchallenged pattern and practice on the ground in domains where citizens act freely and governments lie low.

When we look at the actual pattern of lived rights in America . . . we find lots of regulations of guns, but few outright prohibitions of guns in homes.

Consider, for example, the famous 1965 privacy case *Griswold v. Connecticut*. The state of Connecticut purported to criminalize the use of contraception, even by married couples, prompting the Supreme Court to strike down this extraordinarily intrusive state law as unconstitutional. Writing for the majority, Justice William Douglas claimed that a general right of privacy could be found in between the lines of the Bill of Rights. But Douglas did a poor job of proving his case. It's hard not to smirk when the First Amendment is used to protect the erotic urges of a man and a woman seeking to "assemble" on a bed. Writing separately in *Griswold*, the second Justice John Harlan, widely admired for his judicial care and craftsmanship, offered a more modest and less strained rationale: "Conclusive, in my view, is the utter novelty of [Connecticut's] enactment. Although the Federal Government and many States have at one time or another had on their books statutes forbidding the distribution of contraceptives, none, so far as I can find, has made the use of contraceptives a crime." Thus, the basic practice of the American people rendered Connecticut's oddball law presumptively unconstitutional. It is also highly noteworthy that today around a dozen state constitutions and countless statutes speak explicitly of a right to privacy—a right nowhere explicitly mentioned in the federal Constitution.

Now take Harlan's sensible approach to the unenumerated right of privacy and apply it to Dick Anthony Heller's claim that he has a right to have a gun in his D.C. home for self-defense. When we look at the actual pattern of lived rights in America—what the people have, in fact, done—we find lots of regulations of guns, but few outright prohibitions of guns in homes as sweeping as the D.C. ordinance. We also find a right to keep guns affirmed in a great many modern state constitutions, several of which use the phrase "bear arms" in ways that clearly go beyond the military context. Unlike founding-era documents, modern state constitutions routinely affirm a constitutional right to "bear arms" for hunting, recreation, and/or self-defense.

Support for Gun Rights in the Fourteenth Amendment

In addition to the Ninth Amendment, we should also view the right to bear arms through the lens of the 14th Amendment's command that "No state shall make or enforce any law which shall abridge the privileges or immunities of citizens of the United States." Though this particular sentence applies only to the states, other language in the 14th Amendment affirms that the federal government, too, has a parallel obligation to respect the fundamental rights of citizens.

But the 14th Amendment did not specifically enumerate these sacred privileges and immunities. Instead, like the Ninth, the 14th invited interpreters to pay close attention to fundamental rights that Americans had affirmed through their lived experience—in state bills of rights and in other canonical texts such as the Declaration of Independence and landmark civil rights legislation. And when it came to guns, a companion statute to the 14th Amendment, enacted by Congress in 1866, declared that "laws ... concerning personal liberty [and] personal security ... including the constitutional right to bear arms, shall be secured to and enjoyed by all the citizens." Here, in sharp contrast to founding-era legal texts, the "bear arms" phrase was decisively severed from the military context. Women as well as men could claim a "personal" right to protect their "personal liberty" and "personal security" in their homes. The Reconstruction-era [post-Civil War] Congress clearly understood that Southern blacks might need guns in their homes to protect themselves from private violence in places where they could not rely on local constables to keep their neighborhoods safe. When guns were outlawed, only outlaw Klansmen [members of white supremacy terrorist group Ku Klux Klan] would have guns, to paraphrase a modern NRA [National Rifle Association, a gun rights advocacy group] slogan. In this critical chapter in the history of American liberty, we find additional evidence of an individual right to have a gun in one's home, regardless of the original meaning of the Second Amendment.

Advantages of a New Framework

There are at least three advantages in shifting 21st-century gun-control discourse in this direction. First, a Ninth-and-14th Amendment framework is more modest. Unusually draconian [strict] gun laws can be struck down simply because they lie outside the lived pattern of the American experience, while more mainstream gun laws can be upheld precisely because they have proved acceptable to the people in many places. If our nation's capital wants to argue that specially strict gun rules should apply there because the city faces unique risks, no rigid textual language prevents judges from considering such pragmatic claims in the course of interpreting the boundaries of actual American practice. By contrast, if the Second Amendment's language really did guarantee a right to guns in homes, by what authority could judges allow for a different approach in D.C.? And then, if one has a Second Amendment right to a pistol or shotgun at home, why not a machine gun? Given that the Second Amendment's core right is military, it would seem odd that military arms would be easier to ban than other weapons.

Second, the Ninth and 14th Amendments are more modern and democratically responsive. The Ninth invites us to consider not only rights that have long been part of the American tradition but also rights that have emerged in actual modern practice and in state constitutional clauses of relatively recent vintage that are relatively easy to amend. The 14th directs our attention to the still-relevant problems of race and police protection or the absence thereof. By contrast, the Second Amendment harkens back to a lost 18th-century America, where citizens regularly mustered for militia service on the town square and where the federal army was rightly suspect. This is not our world.

Finally, a focus on the Ninth and 14th Amendments is simply more honest. The open-ended language of the Ninth and 14th Amendments really did aim to invite Americans to ponder state constitutional provisions that declare rights, and these provisions really do focus on individual self-defense. The framers of the 14th Amendment really did focus intently on self-defense in the home. The framers of the Second did not.

The Appeals Court Ruling in *District of Columbia v. Heller* Showed Sound Reasoning

Bob Barr

Bob Barr was a member of the U.S. House of Representatives from 1995 to 2003, and he now runs a consulting firm, Liberty Strategies LLC.

Every once in a while—a long while—a federal court decision comes along that is so lucid and solid it deserves kudos. Thus it is with the decision rendered [in March 2007] by the U.S. Court of Appeals for the District of Columbia, throwing out the 30-year-old Washington, D.C., ban on private ownership of firearms.

While the 2–1 decision [in *Parker v. District of Columbia*, now called *District of Columbia v. Heller* on appeal to the U.S. Supreme Court] directly affects only the District of Columbia, the opinion will likely be widely cited in other jurisdictions. . . . This case may well become the vehicle through which the Supreme Court will, after more than two-and-a-quarter centuries, squarely address the question of whether and to what extent the Second Amendment to the Constitution protects an individual right to keep and bear arms.[1]

The Court's Holding in *Heller*

The case on which . . . [the] seminal opinion was based was brought by six average citizens of the nation's capital. In fact, the parties included a police officer in the District who was

1. On June 26, 2008, the Supreme Court upheld the decision the author is discussing here.

Bob Barr, "Ruling Respects Constitution," *Atlanta Journal Constitution*, March 14, 2007. Reproduced by permission. www.bobbarr2008.com/articles/67/ruling-respects-constitution/.

authorized to carry a handgun while working at the Federal Judicial Center, but was prohibited from keeping a gun at his home.

The District of Columbia was joined in its effort to uphold its anti-firearms law by the Brady gun control organization, and by governors and mayors of many pro-gun control cities and states, including Massachusetts, Maryland, New Jersey, New York City, San Francisco and Chicago. While Eleanor Holmes Norton, the District of Columbia's non-voting delegate in the House of Representatives was vehement in blaming the National Rifle Association [NRA] for the Court of Appeals' decision, the NRA was simply one of a long list. Pro-Second Amendment attorneys general and civil rights organizations filed friend-of-the-court briefs backing the six District of Columbia residents.

The right to arm oneself included the right of self-defense, and was not limited to hunting as some have argued.

The two judges who authored the 58-page majority opinion began and ended their decision with the one-sentence-long Second Amendment to the Constitution of the United States: "A well-regulated Militia, being necessary to the security of a free State, the right of the people to keep and bear Arms shall not be infringed." The jurists quoted liberally from previous court decisions that touched on different aspects of the Second Amendment, and they drew on historical writings and debates surrounding adoption of the amendment. But the judges relied as well on common sense and basic rules of grammar in concluding that:

- The right to keep and bear arms, as a fundamental right of a free people similar to those rights dealt with in other parts of the Bill of Rights, existed independently of and preceded the document in which they were enumerated.

- The right is an individual one as opposed to a collective or civic right.

- The operative clause in the amendment is "the right of the people," and the reference to a "Militia" is merely "prefatory."

- The right to arm oneself included the right of self-defense, and was not limited to hunting as some have argued.

- Handguns clearly were contemplated as being included in the concept of "Arms" in the amendment.

- While the right as guaranteed in the amendment is not absolute, a law that effectively prohibits its exercise cannot be tolerated.

A Narrow Focus

Importantly also, the majority opinion did not attempt to go beyond the specific question presented it. For example, the court did not address the issue of whether D.C. residents have a right to carry firearms outside their homes. This narrow focus of the majority's opinion strengthens its chances for being affirmed on appeal.

The majority did, however, employ unusually strong language in its characterization of the District of Columbia's arguments seeking to have its 1976 anti-gun ordinance upheld based on its opinion that the Second Amendment reflects not an individual right but a collective right limited only to organized "militias" and that handguns were not contemplated as being included in the term "Arms." The majority referred to such arguments by the D.C. government as "outlandish," "strained," and "risible" (that is, "laughable"...).

[The] appeals court opinion certainly does not represent the federal court system's final word on the Second Amendment. However, its clear language and sound reasoning provide hope this unfairly maligned provision in our Bill of Rights finally will be accorded the respect its companion measures have long enjoyed.

Current
CONTROVERSIES

CHAPTER 4

Is Gun
Ownership Dangerous?

Chapter Preface

One of the main arguments offered by gun rights advocates to support their view that U.S. citizens should be permitted to own and use firearms is that they are needed for self-defense. The police, gun supporters say, often arrive only after a violent crime has been committed and thus cannot truly protect people in their homes, cars, or public places from criminals with guns. According to this view, citizens' only real protection if they find themselves the target of a robbery, rape, or homicide is a weapon that allows them to fight back. In many cases, gun advocates argue, just the display of a gun will be enough to deter most criminals and prevent the crime from happening. And if the criminal keeps coming, pro-gun advocates say, then the armed citizen at least has a fighting chance to stop a violent attack. U.S. citizens have always had a legal right to self-defense—that is, the right to defend against criminal prosecution or punishment after the fact if they shoot an assailant. In recent years, however, some states have begun to clarify and in some cases broaden the right of self-defense by adopting so-called "stand-your-ground" laws.

Stand-your-ground laws are based on a traditional legal principle known as the "castle doctrine"—an old notion that "a man's home is his castle." This doctrine holds that if an intruder breaks into a home, the resident can use deadly force if it is reasonably believed that the intruder would inflict serious physical injury. Outside the home, however, most states have traditionally permitted the use of deadly force by citizens only if they were threatened with physical injury and were unable to back away from the criminal. This was known as the "duty to retreat."

Today, as a result of increased citizen concerns about crime, and pressure from gun advocacy groups such as the

National Rifle Association, a number of states have adopted statutes that expand on the traditional citizen rights of self-defense. These stand-your-ground laws typically permit citizens to use deadly force whenever an intruder forcibly enters their home. In addition, many of these new laws allow people to defend themselves with deadly force even in public places and even without the duty to retreat. These new measures are designed to ensure that citizens acting in self-defense will not be held accountable in criminal or civil court for their actions, in some cases even if bystanders are injured.

The first state to take such action was Florida, which enacted a stand-your-ground law in October 2005. Under Florida's law, Florida residents can now use deadly force in their homes, whether they fear physical injury or not. They also can fire on anyone who unlawfully and forcibly enters their home or vehicle, such as a car or a boat, regardless of whether they fear physical assault. Moreover, the Florida law extended self-defense rights to public places; outside the home, Floridians who have a reasonable fear that someone is about to use deadly force against them can now shoot without first attempting to retreat. Enforcement of these new rights, however, comes only after a shooting incident. At that point, local law enforcement will decide based on the facts whether the citizen acted in self-defense. If the facts are unclear or if law enforcement officers believe the citizen acted unreasonably, prosecutors can still charge the resident with a crime and he or she will have to prove the stand-your-ground defense in court. The Florida law also allows citizens to use this defense in civil lawsuits for money damages brought by the person who was shot.

Since the enactment of Florida's law, South Dakota, Indiana, Oklahoma, Michigan, Alabama, Mississippi, Kentucky, and Georgia have passed similar stand-your-ground laws, and Arizona and Idaho have adopted slightly less broad versions. According to gun lobbyists, a number of other states are also considering this type of legislation. Legal experts say many states already permit citizens to shoot intruders in their homes, and at least 38 states allow concealed weapons in public places, so adopting slightly broader stand-your-ground laws may not be such a large step for many areas of the country.

Proponents of stand-your-ground laws claim that they will help with crime control, send a strong warning to would-be criminals, and give ordinary citizens a greater advantage against the bad guys who want to do them harm. Opponents, on the other hand, call the new laws "shoot first" laws and argue that they encourage vigilantism and gang warfare, encourage citizens who may have little knowledge about guns to use them indiscriminately, and increase the risks of bystanders being hurt or killed by guns in public arenas. The issue is really a policy matter about how to cope with crime and gun violence, about which people can disagree, depending on their perspectives. Indeed, the debate about stand-your-ground laws is part of the larger question addressed by the authors of the viewpoints in this chapter—whether gun ownership is dangerous.

Guns in the Home Increase the Risks of Homicides and Suicides

Linda L. Dahlberg, Robin M. Ikeda, and Marcie-jo Kresnow

Linda L. Dahlberg, Robin M. Ikeda, and Marcie-jo Kresnow work for the National Center for Injury Prevention and Control, part of the Centers for Disease Control and Prevention (CDC), which in turn is part of the U.S. Department of Health and Human Services.

Over 50,000 homicides and suicides occur each year in the United States, making them among the leading causes of death, particularly for young people. In 2001, homicide was the second leading cause of death and suicide the third for persons 15–24 years of age. Approximately 60 percent of all homicides and suicides in the United States are committed with a firearm.

Although an estimated 40 percent of adults in the United States report keeping a gun in the home for recreational or protective purposes, the risks and benefits of this practice are widely disputed in the literature. Ecologic analyses [studies that compare groups rather than individuals] have suggested a link between the prevalence of gun ownership and rates of homicide and suicide and between regulations restricting access to firearms and rates of homicide and suicide. Although these studies are useful in demonstrating an association between access to firearms and rates of homicide and suicide at the aggregate level, it is not possible with this methodology to adequately assess whether access to a gun increases the risk of a violent death at the individual level. . . .

Linda L. Dahlberg, Robin M. Ikeda, and Marcie-jo Kresnow, "Guns in the Home and Risk of a Violent Death in the Home: Findings from a National Study," *American Journal of Epidemiology*, June 7, 2004. Reproduced by permission.

To evaluate the relation between firearms in the home and violent deaths in the home, we analyzed data from a US mortality follow-back survey. The purpose of our study was two-fold: 1) to determine whether having a firearm in the home increases the risk of a homicide or suicide in the home relative to other causes of death in the home, and 2) to determine whether having a firearm in the home increases the risk that a homicide or suicide in the home will be committed with a firearm or by using other means. To our knowledge, this is the first national study to specifically examine the relation between firearms and violent deaths in the home. . . .

Nearly three quarters of suicide victims lived in a home where one or more firearms were present, compared with 42 percent of homicide victims.

Findings

[Our study found that] homicide victims were mostly male, less than 35 years of age, and of racial or ethnic minority status. Suicide victims were predominately male, older, and non-Hispanic White. There was a slightly higher proportion of males among persons who died of other causes. These decedents were also mostly older than 45 years of age and non-Hispanic White. Although a large proportion of homicide victims had never married, most of the suicide victims and persons who died of other causes were married at the time of death or had been previously married. The majority of decedents, regardless of cause of death, were living with other people at the time of death. A large proportion of both homicide and suicide victims died in the southern region of the United States.

Nearly three quarters of suicide victims lived in a home where one or more firearms were present, compared with 42 percent of homicide victims and one third of those who died of other causes. A firearm was used in 68 percent of both homicides and suicides. A larger proportion of homicide decedents than suicide decedents and those who died of other causes were drinking alcohol within 4 hours of death and used illicit drugs in the past year. A larger proportion of suicide decedents than homicide decedents and those who died of other causes expressed a wish to die, suicidal ideation [thinking], and symptoms of depression and anxiety in the last month of life.

Over three quarters (76.3 percent) of the homicide victims knew their assailant. Nearly one third (31.7 percent) of the homicides occurred during a family argument, 15.4 percent during a robbery, 4.1 percent during a drug deal, 0.2 percent during an abduction, and 44.1 percent for other unspecified reasons. In 4.5 percent of the homicides, multiple circumstances were reported. . . .

There was a significant sex-by-gun-in-the-home interaction for suicide. Males with firearms in the home were at a significantly greater risk of suicide than males without guns in the home. Females with firearms in the home were also at an elevated risk of suicide compared with females without guns in the home, but the difference was only borderline significant. Other important predictors of suicide risk included young age (<35 years), suicidal ideation, and symptoms of depression and anxiety in the last month of life. Living alone was borderline significant. . . .

Among those living alone at the time of death, there was no association between the presence of a firearm in the home and method of homicide. However, for persons living with others at the time of death, there was a significant association between the presence of a firearm in the home and risk of a firearm homicide among those aged 35 years or older. We found no significant interactions in the model for suicide. Those persons with guns in the home were at significantly greater risk than those without guns in the home of dying from a firearm suicide versus one committed by using other means. No variables other than a firearm in the home were important predictors of firearm homicide. In addition to a gun in the home, male sex and living in the South were important predictors of firearm suicide. . . .

Those persons with guns in the home, regardless of the type of gun, number of guns, or storage practice, were at significantly greater risk of dying from a firearm homicide and firearm suicide than those without guns in the home. There were no significant differences between those with only handguns in the home and those with only long guns or both handguns and long guns, those with two or more guns, and those having one gun in the household; and between those who stored one or more guns unlocked and those who stored all guns locked.

A Strong Link Between Guns and Violent Death in the Home

The findings of this study add to the body of research showing an association between guns in the home and risk of a violent death. Those persons with guns in the home were at significantly greater risk than those without guns in the home of dying from a suicide in the home relative to other causes of death. This finding was particularly the case for males, who in general have higher rates of completed suicide than females do. The findings showing an increased risk of homicide in homes with guns are also consistent with previous research, although, when compared with suicide, are not as strong. . . .

Our findings also suggest that the presence of a gun in the home increases the chance that a homicide or suicide in the home will be committed with a firearm rather than by using other means. Victims of suicide living in homes with guns were more than 30 times more likely to have died from a firearm-related suicide than from one committed with a different method. Guns are highly lethal, require little preparation, and may be chosen over less lethal methods to commit suicide, particularly when the suicide is impulsive. Suicidal persons may also be more likely to acquire a gun to commit suicide and, given the lethality of the weapon, are more likely to complete suicide, although the evidence on this point is mixed.

For victims of homicide, there was also a strong association between guns in the home and risk of dying from a firearm-related homicide, but this risk varied by age and whether the person was living with others at the time of death. These deaths may have been related to domestic violence or to other interpersonal disputes either involving them or someone else in the household. The majority of victims knew their assailant, suggesting that the assailant was either a family member or was acquainted with the victim or victim's family and less likely to be an unknown intruder.

Some of the research conducted to date has found a higher risk of a violent death in homes with handguns and unlocked and loaded guns. However, many studies have either not examined the risk associated with specific firearm-related characteristics (e.g., type of gun or storage practice) or have found no significant differences. In our study, the risk of dying from a firearm-related homicide or suicide was greater in homes with guns, but this risk did not vary by specific firearm-related characteristics. Simply having a gun in the home increased the risk of a firearm homicide or firearm suicide in the home. Whether certain types of guns or storage practices confer greater or lesser risk, or reflect recall and reporting biases when studied, is unclear. Previous research suggests that proxy respondents and nonusers of firearms are not always knowledgeable about the number or types of guns in the household or the storage practice and may be inclined to give socially desirable responses. . . .

Much of the debate in the literature has focused on the risks and benefits of gun ownership in terms of lives saved versus lives harmed. Studies of defensive gun use suggest that millions of defensive gun use incidents occur each year by people to protect themselves or their property against assaults, theft, or break-ins. However, guns are also involved in unintentional firearm shootings and domestic altercations in the home and are the primary method used in suicides in the United States. The body of research to date, including the findings of this study, shows a strong association between guns in the home and risk of suicide. The findings for homicide, while showing an elevated risk, have consistently been more modest.

Guns in the Home Pose a Risk for Children

Alan L. Hammond

Alan L. Hammond is a writer from Lexington, Kentucky.

The thought of an unsupervised child with a firearm is bone chilling. Proper gun safety can reduce, but not eliminate unthinkable gun accidents. Child-safety and gun-ownership are terms that don't seem to fit together. It should go without saying, with guns at home, adequate safety precautions are paramount. It is surely one time when the right to keep and bear arms should be, to an extent, "self-infringed." Here are some ways to help ensure a peaceful co-existence between children and guns.

Removing the Guns

Get them out of the house! The guns, that is. Since 100% safety is the goal, then this is the only way to ensure the worst doesn't happen. Parents know children are always observing, even when they don't appear to be. Given enough time, the child may be found spinning a revolver's cylinder, showing neighbors the hunting rifle scope (which was removed from the well-hidden rifle), and building a tower with shotgun shells. Those are the best things that can come from guns in the home. It's a huge, horrible leap to the next set of possibilities.

Firearm Safety Precautions

Should the decision be made to keep firearms at home, go overboard with safety. First, guns should remain unloaded. Safe gun owners are careful to unload when they leave the field, the practice range, the forest. They should be no less careful when storing the weapons at home. Unless the home is entrenched in a militarized zone, there is no reason to keep a loaded firearm "handy." The chances of a child being killed by that loaded weapon is infinitely more likely than the gun being used to stop a kidnapper, murderer or prison escapee up to no good.

Ammunition should be kept in a location separate from the firearms. An unloaded gun stored with its ammunition might as well be loaded. If the two are stored together, even a toddler can make the connection of where and how the bullet goes in the gun.

Next, keep them both securely locked away. Store weapons and ammunition apart from one another, in locked cabinets. At the very least, in a cabinet secured by a lock and key. At best, in a combination-lock secured gun safe or gun cabinet. If firearms are secured by a padlock with a key, the children will find the key and let their curiosity take over from there. With a combination-lock safe, preferably one without a key backup, the combination can be committed to memory and, short of hiring a locksmith, the children won't have access to the contents. Again, it may seem extreme, but without ammunition, the guns won't fire.

Gun owners should be exceedingly cautious and thorough when educating their children on the dangers of firearms.

If that seems overboard, then the additional feature of trigger locks will seem outrageous. So far, the gun lies unloaded, apart from its ammunition, inside a safe, behind a combination lock. Most gun-related injuries are caused by accidents involving "unloaded" guns, those previously thought to be unloaded. Placing a trigger lock on the unloaded weapon before bringing it home, either after a hunt or straight from the firearms dealer will help prevent such accidents. Trigger locks are inexpensive and can be found at most large department stores, sporting goods stores and firearms dealers.

Perceptive Children

Children will watch how parents handle guns. If parents are careless with weapons, should a child ever get their hands on it, they will mimic those actions. Parents who handle guns with respect and care will impart the same habit to their children. Actions, backed by spoken procedures for handling and care, will add a layer of protection against ever present danger.

Gun owners should be exceedingly cautious and thorough when educating their children on the dangers of firearms. The right to own a firearm is a prized freedom, but when children are present, parents should impose their own restrictions on that right. The consequences of not doing so are inconceivable.

Guns Save Lives

John Stossel

John Stossel is co-anchor of the ABC News *television show* 20/20 *and the author of the book* Myth, Lies, and Downright Stupidity.

It's all too predictable. A day after a gunman killed six people and wounded 18 others at Northern Illinois University, *The New York Times* criticized the U.S. Interior Department for preparing to rethink its ban on guns in national parks. The editorial board wants "the 51 senators who like the thought of guns in the parks—and everywhere else, it seems—to realize that the innocence of Americans is better protected by carefully controlling guns than it is by arming everyone to the teeth."

Laws Against Self-Defense

As usual, the *Times* editors seem unaware of how silly their argument is. To them, the choice is between "carefully controlling guns" and "arming everyone to the teeth." But no one favors "arming everyone to the teeth" (whatever that means). Instead, gun advocates favor freedom, choice and self-responsibility. If someone wishes to be prepared to defend himself, he should be free to do so. No one has the right to deprive others of the means of effective self-defense, like a handgun.

As for the first option, "carefully controlling guns," how many shootings at schools or malls will it take before we understand that people who intend to kill are not deterred by gun laws? Last I checked, murder is against the law everywhere. No one intent on murder will be stopped by the prospect of committing a lesser crime like illegal possession of a firearm. The intellectuals and politicians who make pious declarations about controlling guns should explain how their gunless utopia is to be realized. While they search for—excuse me—their magic bullet, innocent people are dying defenseless.

That's because laws that make it difficult or impossible to carry a concealed handgun do deter one group of people: law-abiding citizens who might have used a gun to stop crime. Gun laws are laws against self-defense.

Criminals have the initiative. They choose the time, place and manner of their crimes, and they tend to make choices that maximize their own, not their victims', success. So criminals don't attack people they know are armed, and anyone thinking of committing mass murder is likely to be attracted to a gun-free zone, such as schools and malls.

Guns—The First Line of Defense

Government may promise to protect us from criminals, but it cannot deliver on that promise. This was neatly summed up in a book title a few years ago: *Dial 911 and Die.* If you are the target of a crime, only one other person besides the criminal is sure to be on the scene: you. There is no good substitute for self-responsibility.

How, then, does it make sense to create mandatory gun-free zones, which in reality are free-crime zones?

The usual suspects keep calling for more gun control laws. But this idea that gun control is crime control is just a myth. The National Academy of Sciences reviewed dozens of studies and could not find a single gun regulation that clearly led to reduced violent crime or murder. When Washington, D.C., passed its tough handgun ban years ago, gun violence rose.

The press ignores the fact that often guns save lives. It's what happened in 2002 at the Appalachian School of Law [in Grundy, Virginia]. Hearing shots, two students went to their cars, got their guns and restrained the shooter until police arrested him.

Likewise, law professor Glenn Reynolds writes, "Pearl, Miss., school shooter Luke Woodham was stopped when the school's vice principal took a .45 from his truck and ran to the scene. In [the 2007] Utah mall shooting, it was an off-duty police officer who happened to be on the scene and carrying a gun."

It's impossible to know exactly how often guns stop criminals. Would-be victims don't usually report crimes that don't happen. But people use guns in self-defense every day. The [libertarian think tank] Cato Institute's Tom Palmer says just showing his gun to muggers once saved his life. "It equalizes unequals," Palmer told [the television show] *20/20*. "If someone gets into your house, which would you rather have, a handgun or a telephone? You can call the police if you want, and they'll get there, and they'll take a picture of your dead body. But they can't get there in time to save your life. The first line of defense is you."

Rural Homeowners Need Guns for Self-Defense

Massad Ayoob

Massad Ayoob is a firearms and self-defense instructor, a writer, and the director of the Lethal Force Institute in Concord, New Hampshire.

Do rural homeowners need guns for self-defense? Sometimes they do and sometimes they don't, . . . but those who did never really knew they would until it happened.

Crime in Rural Areas

I've spent a lot of time running with big-city cops to learn lessons from them, but I've never been one myself. I was always a small town officer. I spent eight years at one growing town that was next to the state's biggest city, but also had remote corners that were virtually Appalachian. The second was a genuine rural community a couple of towns over from the first one, where I did two years as sergeant and six as lieutenant. In the eleven years since, I've served a genuinely rural small municipality that would be even more blessedly quiet were it not for an interstate highway passing through it that's a drug conduit from Montreal to the Boston and New York metroplexes. Moreover, I've done it all as a part-time cop with full arrest power and rank authority, a few hundred hours a year; what I do full time is teach this stuff. This may be why [I was picked] to write this column, instead of a big city career cop. One of the big reasons people give up the city lifestyle or the 'burbs for a "Backwoods Home" is their perception that they'll be safe from crime. Don't bet on it. The bad guys in the cities you fled or want to flee figured out a long

Massad Ayoob, "Do Rural Homeowners Need Guns for Self-Defense?" *Backwoods Home Magazine*, June 4, 2008. Reproduced by permission.

time ago that the "Thin Blue Line" [police force] is thinnest in the hinterlands. America is the society that is interconnected by interstate highways. Most of us in rural law enforcement have very strong reason to believe that a lot of burglary and violent crime in our provinces is done by out of town city punks who don't want to crap where they live. Sure, we have our indigenous country scumbags, but we can generally stay on top of them and take care of them expeditiously.

The overwhelming majority of encounters between armed citizens and violent criminals end . . . [with the perpetrator fleeing or surrendering].

Let me tell you a true story from a long time ago. I was a young patrolman on the rural edge of that first community I told you about. I wrote about it in a book called *In the Gravest Extreme* when the memory was a lot fresher in my mind, so let me quote from that now.

The call came over the radio and I hit the lights and siren. A drug-crazed suspect had forced his way into a suburban home on the edge of the community I patrolled.

He was gone when we got there, but he had already left a residue of fear that would never go away. He'd had the wife down on her living room couch when the husband, hearing her screams, grabbed his Walther .32 auto from his night-table drawer and ran to her aid.

The guy heard him coming, and threw himself to his feet to take the husband. The guy was big. Then he saw the pistol . . . and got small.

He backed out the door screaming threats, covering his face like a vampire in a late-show movie cringing from a crucifix. By the time the husband had chased him out, his wife had run to the bedroom closet and fetched the loaded 12-

gauge. As the druggie stood on the lawn screaming obscene threats at the homeowner, the latter fired a round of bird-shot into the air, and the attacker fled into the woods.

During the hours that followed, as I and a contingent of brother officers stalked the suspect through the woods, I reflected on the value of that little .32 automatic in that man's night-table drawer. We'd had a decent response time—we were on the scene less than a minute after getting the hysterical phone call—but as I crept through the pitch-black woods that night, listening to the sound of the bloodhounds, I couldn't help but wonder what might have happened if he hadn't had that little gun. I admit, I didn't reflect on it too much at the time, because I was more preoccupied with the sounds and movements around me as I still-hunted the brush with a Kel-Lite flashlight going on-and-off in one hand, and a Colt .45 automatic in the other. But I knew damn well that without the little .32, we might not have gotten the call until it was too late.

Later that night, when the thing was (bloodlessly) ended, that man came up to me and said, "Officer, my wife is afraid they're going to arrest me for threatening him with a gun. They aren't, are they?"

I put my hand on the guy's shoulder. I told him he wouldn't be arrested. I told him to come in to the police station Monday morning and see about getting a "carry" pistol permit. And then I gave him the address of a friend of mine who runs a police equipment shop, and promised him a discount on something bigger than a .32 automatic. Somewhere in between came a lecture on trusting the frail hook-and-eye lock on his screen door.

That was then. This is now. Little has changed.

The citizen in that incident was about my age, then. With all the intervening years, he could have died of old age. I hope not. But if he is gone, I hope it was old age. An old age the loaded guns he kept where he and his wife could reach them bought for them both.

A Skill You Need Desperately

The overwhelming majority of encounters between armed citizens and violent criminals end just that way, whether in the depths of the inner city or in the wilderness. Perpetrator begins to attack. Perpetrator sees gun pointing at him. Perpetrator suddenly decides that he has made a terrible mistake, and is about to die from what I've come to call "sudden and acute failure of the victim selection process." Perpetrator either flees or surrenders. End of story. Most of the time. Sometimes, the predator is so obsessed or enraged, so drugged out or drunk, or just so unbelievably stupid that he continues the attack. When this happens, the citizen/victim has no choice but to steady the gun and pull the trigger. This is the moment at which you will need not only the wherewithal to do what needs to be done, but the skill and familiarity with the firearm to allow you to do so.

The great defensive handgun expert Jeff Cooper once said that combat shooting training and practice was akin to lifeboat drills on an ocean liner. It was, one hoped, the last skill you would ever have to employ during your journey. But, if you did need it, it would be a skill you needed desperately.

Let's go back for a minute to the story I recounted earlier, from the 1970s. I'm proud to say that the police response time was fast for a metropolitan department, let alone for a small community. Quick question, though: in your now or future backwoods home, how long will it take the police to respond once you call them from your remote location? And go back to that true story one more time: if that peaceful rural home had not been armed, would either the husband or the wife have been able to make the call at all?

About the time you read this [June 2008], two teenage males in a community very close to the one my department serves will go on trial for the murder of a respected middle-aged couple who lived in a somewhat remote home. Neither was able to access a gun to prevent being brutally butchered by assailants armed with combat knives. They thought they lived in a safe place where people didn't need guns, right up until they were hacked to death in a bloodbath that exceeded the [1971 Stanley Kubrick] *Clockwork Orange* movie.

Owning and responsibly keeping a firearm, and knowing how and when to use it defensively if you must, is your choice. But so is participating in the lifeboat drills when you're on that ocean cruise. The ones who needed the lifeboat were always glad they spent the time preparing. The ones who practiced and didn't need it still achieved peace of mind.

But, as always, the choice is yours.

The Media Underestimates the Defensive Uses of Guns

Larry Elder

Larry Elder is a nationally syndicated libertarian talk show host on KABC in Los Angeles.

Forty-six-year-old Joyce Cordoba stood behind the deli counter while working at a Wal-Mart in Albuquerque, New Mexico. Suddenly, her ex-husband—against whom Ms. Cordoba had a restraining order—showed up, jumped over the deli counter, and began stabbing Ms. Cordoba. Due Moore, a 72-year-old Wal-Mart customer, witnessed the violent attack. Moore, legally permitted to carry a concealed weapon, pulled out his gun, and shot and killed the ex-husband. Ms. Cordoba survived the brutal attack and is recovering from her wounds.

We know that in 2003, 12,548 people died through non-suicide gun violence, including homicides, accidents, and cases of undetermined intent. This raises a question: How often do Americans use guns for defensive purposes?

The Defensive Use of Guns

UCLA professor emeritus James Q. Wilson, a respected expert on crime, police practices, and guns, says, "We know from Census Bureau surveys that something beyond a hundred thousand uses of guns for self-defense occur every year. We know from smaller surveys of a commercial nature that the number may be as high as two-and-a-half or three million. We don't know what the right number is, but whatever the right number is, it's not a trivial number."

Criminologist and researcher Gary Kleck, using his own commissioned phone surveys and number extrapolation, estimates that 2.5 million Americans use guns for defensive purposes each year. He further found that of those who had used guns defensively, one in six believed someone would have been dead if they had not resorted to their defensive use of firearms. That corresponds to approximately 400,000 of Kleck's estimated 2.5 million defensive gun uses. Kleck points out that if only one-tenth of the people were right about saving a life, the number of people saved annually by guns would still be at least 40,000.

The Department of Justice's own National Institute of Justice (NIJ) study titled "Guns in America: National Survey on Private Ownership and Use of Firearms" estimated that 1.5 million Americans use guns for defensive purposes every year. Although the government's figure estimated a million fewer people defensively using guns, the NIJ called their figure "directly comparable" to Kleck's, noting that "it is statistically plausible that the difference is due to sampling error." Furthermore, the NIJ reported that half of their respondents who said they used a gun defensively also admitted having done so multiple times a year—making the number of estimated uses of self-defense with a gun 4.7 million times annually.

Former assistant district attorney and firearms expert David Kopel writes, "[W]hen a robbery victim does not defend himself, the robber succeeds 88 percent of the time, and the victim is injured 25 percent of the time. When a victim resists with a gun, the robbery success rate falls to 30 percent, and the victim injury rate falls to 17 percent. No other response to a robbery—from drawing a knife to shouting for help to fleeing—produces such low rates of victim injury and robbery success."

The Anti-Gun Media Bias

What do "gun control activists" say? The Brady Center to Prevent Gun Violence's website displays this oft-quoted "fact": "The risk of homicide in the home is three times greater in households with guns." Their website fails to mention, however, that Dr. Arthur Kellermann, the "expert" who came up with that figure, later backpedaled after others discredited his studies for failing to follow standard scientific procedures.

Americans, in part due to mainstream media's anti-gun bias, dramatically underestimate the defensive uses of guns.

According to *The Wall Street Journal*, Dr. Kellermann now concedes, "A gun can be used to scare away an intruder without a shot being fired," admitting that he failed to include such events in his original study. "Simply keeping a gun in the home," Kellermann says, "may deter some criminals who fear confronting an armed homeowner." He adds, "It is possible that reverse causation accounted for some of the association we observed between gun ownership and homicide—i.e., in a limited number of cases, people may have acquired a gun in response to a specific threat."

More Guns, Less Crime author John Lott points out that, in general, our mainstream media fails to inform the public about defensive uses of guns. "Hardly a day seems to go by," writes Lott, "without national news coverage of yet another shooting. Yet when was the last time you heard a story on the national evening news about a citizen saving a life with a gun? . . . An innocent person's murder is more newsworthy than when a victim brandishes a gun and an attacker runs away with no crime committed . . . [B]ad events provide emotionally gripping pictures. Yet covering only the bad events creates the impression that guns only cost lives."

Americans, in part due to mainstream media's anti-gun bias, dramatically underestimate the defensive uses of guns. Some, after using a gun for self-defense, fear that the police may charge them for violating some law or ordinance about firearm possession and use. So many Americans simply do not tell the authorities.

A gunned-down bleeding guy creates news. A man who spared his family by brandishing a handgun, well, that's just water-cooler chat.

Organizations to Contact

The editors have compiled the following list of organizations concerned with the issues debated in this book. The descriptions are derived from materials provided by the organizations. All have publications or information available for interested readers. The list was compiled on the date of publication of the present volume; the information provided here may change. Readers need to remember that many organizations take several weeks or longer to respond to inquiries.

American Civil Liberties Union (ACLU)
125 Broad St., 18th Floor, New York, NY   10004
(212) 549-2500 • fax: (212) 869-9065
e-mail: aclu@aclu.org
Web site: www.aclu.org

The ACLU defends the rights and principles delineated in the Declaration of Independence and the U.S. Constitution. It claims to be neutral on the issue of gun control; however, it takes the position that the Second Amendment does not confer an unlimited right upon individuals to own guns or other weapons, and that it does not prohibit reasonable regulation of gun ownership, such as licensing and registration. The ACLU Web site contains a position statement on this interpretation of the Second Amendment.

Brady Center to Prevent Gun Violence
1225 Eye St. NW, Suite 1100, Washington, DC   20005
(202) 289-7319 • fax: (202) 408-1851
Web site: www.bradycenter.org

The Brady Center is a nonpartisan, grassroots organization for preventing gun violence. Through the Brady Campaign and its network of Million Mom March chapters, this group supports gun control laws, regulations, and public policies, and works to educate the public about gun violence. Its Web site features a number of fact sheets and reports about U.S. gun-related laws, issues, politics, deaths, and injuries.

Cato Institute
1000 Massachusetts Ave. NW, Washington, DC   20001
(202) 842-0200 • fax: (202) 842-3290
e-mail: cato@cato.org
Web site: www.cato.org

The Cato Institute is a libertarian public policy research foundation dedicated to limiting the role of government and protecting individual liberties. Its publications include the Cato Policy Analysis series of reports, which have covered topics such as "Fighting Back: Crime, Self-Defense, and the Right to Carry a Handgun," and "Trust the People: The Case Against Gun Control." It also publishes the magazine *Regulation*, the *Cato Policy Report*, and various studies.

Citizens Committee for the Right to Keep and Bear Arms
12500 NE 10th Pl., Bellevue, WA   98005
(800) 486-6963 • fax: (425) 451-3959
e-mail: info@ccrkba.org
Web site: www.ccrkba.org

The committee believes that the U.S. Constitution's Second Amendment guarantees and protects the right of individual Americans to own guns. It works to educate the public concerning this right and lobbies legislators to prevent the passage of gun-control laws. The committee is affiliated with the Second Amendment Foundation (see below). Its Web site offers press releases and reports on its activities. It also tracks legislation on gun control issues.

Coalition to Stop Gun Violence (CSGV)
1424 L St. NW, Suite 2-1, Washington, DC   20005
(202) 408-0061
e-mail: csgv@csgv.org
Web site: www.csgv.org

The CSGV is a coalition of 45 national organizations, including religious organizations, child welfare advocates, public health professionals, and social justice groups, working to reduce gun violence. The CSGV advocates a progressive agenda to reduce firearm death and injury, and aims to defeat the gun lobby through a strategy that encompasses legislation, litigation, and grassroots efforts. Its Web site offers information on illegal gun markets, the international arms trade, and the subject of guns and democracy.

Gun Owners of America (GOA)

8001 Forbes Pl., Suite 102, Springfield, VA   22151
(703) 321-8585 • fax: (703) 321-8408
e-mail: goamail@gunowners.org
Web site: www.gunowners.org

Gun Owners of America lobbies to preserve and defend the Second Amendment rights of gun owners. The GOA sees firearm ownership as a freedom issue, and represents the views of gun owners whenever the right to bear arms is threatened on a local, state, or national level. The GOA Web site publishes a newsletter, *The Gun Owners.*

Independence Institute

14142 Denver West Pkwy., Suite 101, Golden, CO   80401
(303) 279-6536 • fax: (303) 279-4176
Web site: www.i2i.org

The Independence Institute is a libertarian think tank that supports gun ownership as a civil liberty and a constitutional right. Its Web site features a Second Amendment Project where the reader can find publications opposing gun control, such as the Institute's brief in the *District of Columbia v. Heller* case and articles, fact sheets, and commentary from a variety of sources.

International Action Network on Small Arms (IANSA)
56-64, Leonard Street, London   EC2A 4LT
  England
+44 207 065 0870 • fax: +44 207 065 0871
e-mail: contact@iansa.org
Web site: www.iansa.org

The International Action Network on Small Arms is a network of 700 organizations working in 100 countries to stop the proliferation and misuse of small arms and light weapons. IANSA seeks to make people safer from gun violence by securing stronger regulations on guns in society and better controls on arms exports. Its Web site provides a variety of resources and fact sheets on gun violence.

Jews for the Preservation of Firearms Ownership (JPFO)
PO Box 270143, Hartford, WI   53207
(262) 673-9745 • fax: (262) 673-9746
e-mail: jpfo@jpfo.org
Web site: www.jpfo.org

JPFO is an educational organization that believes Jewish law mandates self-defense. Its primary goal is the elimination of the idea that gun control is a socially useful public policy in any country. JPFO's Web site is a source for anti-gun-control commentary from various sources on firearms and the Second Amendment.

National Crime Prevention Council (NCPC)
2345 Crystal Dr., Suite 500, Arlington, VA   22202
(202) 466-6272 • fax: (202) 296-1356
Web site: www.ncpc.org

The National Crime Prevention Council is an educational nonprofit organization whose mission is to enable people to create safer and more caring communities by addressing the causes of crime and violence and reducing the opportunities for crime to occur. It provides readers with information on gun control and gun violence. The NCPC's publications include the newsletter *Catalyst*, the book *Reducing Gun Violence: What Communities Can Do,* and articles such as "Preventing Youth Weapons Use."

National Institute of Justice (NIJ)
Box 6000, Rockville, MD   20849
(800) 851-3420 • fax: (301) 519-5212
Web site: www.ncjrs.gov

A component of the Office of Justice Programs of the U.S. Department of Justice, the NIJ supports research on crime, criminal behavior, and crime prevention; the National Criminal Justice Reference Service (NCJRS) acts as a clearinghouse that provides information and research about criminal justice. Among the publications available on the NCJRS Web site are research briefs such as "Juvenile Crime in Washington, DC" and "Promising Strategies to Reduce Gun Violence."

National Rifle Association (NRA)
11250 Waples Mill Road, Fairfax, VA   22030
(800) 672-3888
Web site: www.nra.org

The NRA is a powerful pro-gun rights group in the United States. It offers firearm training and other programs in an effort to foster the safe and responsible ownership and use of firearms. Its Web site features articles and links supportive of gun rights as well as information on gun-safety programs and training opportunities. The NRA provides information on firearm-related legislation and politics. Among its publications are the journals *American Rifleman, American Hunter,* and *America's 1⁰ Freedom.*

Project Safe Neighborhoods
U.S. Department of Justice, Washington, DC   20530-0001
(202) 514-2000
e-mail: AskPSN@usdoj.gov
Web site: www.psn.gov

Project Safe Neighborhoods links together federal, state, and local law enforcement, prosecutors, and community leaders to enact a multifaceted approach to deterring and punishing gun crime. It is made up of a network of existing local programs that target gun crime. The Project Safe Neighborhoods program provides funding and additional tools to support these organizations and their endeavors. Its Web site is a source of various government publications relating to gun violence, such as "Report to the President on Issues Raised by the Virginia Tech Tragedy," "Background Checks for Firearm Transfers, 2005," and "Criminal Victimization, 2005."

Second Amendment Committee

PO Box 1776, Hanford, CA   93232
(559) 584-5209 • fax: (559) 584-4084
e-mail: liberty89@libertygunrights.com
Web site: www.libertygunrights.com

The Second Amendment Committee was founded by gun-rights activist Bernadine Smith. The committee supports the role of citizen militias, and its founder has authored legislation promoting state enforcement of the Second Amendment. The organization's Web site provides access to about 700 articles on various topics relating to the right to bear arms.

Second Amendment Foundation (SAF)

12500 NE 10th Pl., Bellevue, WA   98005
(800) 426-4302 • fax: (425) 451-3959
e-mail: AdminForWeb@saf.org
Web site: www.saf.org

The Second Amendment Foundation is dedicated to promoting a better understanding of the right to privately own and possess firearms. It conducts many educational and legal-action programs designed to better inform the public about the gun control debate. The foundation's Web site features gun-rights resources and a list of sponsored publications, including the periodicals *Gun Week* and *Women & Guns*.

Stop Handgun Violence (SHV)
One Bridge St., Suite 300, Newton, MA   02458
(877) SAFE ARMS • fax: (617) 965-7308
e-mail: shv@stophandgunviolence.com
Web site: www.stophandgunviolence.com

Stop Handgun Violence is a nonprofit organization committed to the prevention of gun violence without banning guns: through education, public awareness, effective law enforcement, and common-sense gun laws. SHV has distributed over 30,000 trigger locks to gun owners across the country, and has worked to establish gun-violence prevention curricula in schools across the state of Massachusetts. The group's Web site includes stories about children and guns, gun-violence statistics, gun-violence prevention tips, and information about gun laws.

Violence Policy Center
1730 Rhode Island Ave. NW, Suite 1014
Washington, DC   20036
(202) 822-8200 • fax: (202) 822-8202
Web site: www.vpc.org

The Violence Policy Center is an educational foundation that conducts research on firearms violence. It works to educate the public on the dangers of guns and supports gun control measures. The center's many publications include *American Roulette: Murder-Suicide in the United States*, *Black Homicide Victimization in the United States: An Analysis of 2005 Homicide Data*, and *Drive-By America*.

Bibliography

Books

Akhil Reed Amar   *America's Constitution: A Biography.* New York: Random House, 2005.

Dewey G. Cornell   *School Violence: Fears Versus Facts.* New York: Routledge, 2006.

Saul Cornell   *A Well-Regulated Militia: The Founding Fathers and the Origins of Gun Control in America.* New York: Oxford University Press, 2006.

Wendy Cukier and Victor W. Sidel   *The Global Gun Epidemic: From Saturday Night Specials to AK-47s.* New York: Praeger, 2005.

Alexander DeConde   *Gun Violence in America: The Struggle for Control.* Boston, MA: Northeastern University Press, 2003.

Richard Feldman   *Ricochet: Confessions of a Gun Lobbyist.* Hoboken, NJ: Wiley, 2007.

Daniel Friedman   *Saving Our Children: An In-Depth Look at Gun Violence in Our Nation and Our Schools.* Bloomington, IN: Authorhouse, 2006.

Gary Kleck   *Point Blank: Guns and Violence in America.* Piscataway, NJ: Aldine Transaction, 2005.

John R. Lott Jr. *The Bias Against Guns: Why Almost Everything You've Heard About Gun Control Is Wrong.* Washington, DC: Regnery Publishing, 2003.

Jens Ludwig and Philip J. Cook *Evaluating Gun Policy: Effects on Crime and Violence.* Washington, DC: Brookings Institution Press, 2003.

Robert J. Spitzer *The Politics of Gun Control.* Washington, DC: CQ Press, 2007.

Mark V. Tushnet *Out of Range: Why the Constitution Can't End the Battle Over Guns.* New York: Oxford University Press, 2007.

Periodicals

Steve Chapman "Misfire on Gun Violence," *Washington Times*, April 26, 2008. www.washingtontimes.com/news/2008/apr/26/misfire-on-gun-violence/.

G. D. Curfman, S. Morrissey, J. M. Drazen "Handgun Violence, Public Health, and the Law," *New England Journal of Medicine*, Vol. 358, pp. 1503–1504, 2008.

Linda Greenhouse "Do You Have a Right to 'Bear Arms'?: In the More than 200 Years Since the Adoption of the Bill of Rights, the Supreme Court Has Never Ruled on What the Second Amendment Really Means," *New York Times Upfront*, January 14, 2008.

William P. Hoar   "Does the Second Amendment Apply to D.C.?" *The New American*, August 20, 2007.

International Labour Organization   "New Forms of Violence at Work on the Rise Worldwide, Says the ILO," June 14, 2006. www.ilo.org/global/ About_the_ILO/ Media_and_public_information/ Press_releases/lang--en/ WCMS_070505/index.htm.

Josh Kraushaar   "Ron Paul: More Guns Will Deter Shootings," *Politico.com*, April 17, 2007. www.politico.com/news/stories/ 0407/3556.html.

Dahlia Lithwick   "When Reason Meets Rifles," *Newsweek*, May 24, 2008. www.newsweek.com/id/123509/ page/2.

John R. Lott Jr. and Eli Lehrer   "More Gun Control Isn't the Answer," *American Daily*, June 16, 2004. www.americandaily.com/article/1340.

Joann Loviglio   "Gun Violence's Toll: $100 Billion," *Associated Press*, February 28, 2008.

Joyce Lee Malcolm   "Gun Control's Twisted Outcome," *Reason*, November 2002. www.reason.com/news/show/ 28582.html.

Jim Panyard

"It's Not the Guns, Governor: It's the People," *PennPatriot Blog*, November 20, 2007. http://pennpatriot.blogspot.com/2007/11/its-not-guns-governor-its-people.html.

Jonathan Rauch

"The Right Kind of Gun Rights: Why the D.C. Case Is About Self Defense," *Reason*, March 19, 2008. www.reason.com/news/show/125584.html.

Sacramento [CA] *Bee*

"Editorial: Sick of Gun Violence? Blame Congress, Not Cities," August 14, 2007.

Emma Schwartz

"A Key Case on Gun Control," *U.S. News & World Report*, March 6, 2008. www.usnews.com/articles/news/national/2008/03/06/a-key-case-on-gun-control.html.

———

"In Congress, the Uphill Battle for Gun Control," *U.S. News & World Report*, March 6, 2008. www.usnews.com/articles/news/politics/2008/03/06/in-congress-the-uphill-battle-for-gun-control.html.

Jeff Snyder

"Violence and Nonviolence," *American Handgunner*, July–August 2007.

John Stossel

"Gun Control Isn't Crime Control," *New York Sun*, February 27, 2008. www.nysun.com/opinion/gun-control-isnt-crime-control/71908/.

Jonathan Turley   "A Liberal's Lament: The NRA Might
                         Be Right After All," *USAToday.com*,
                         October 4, 2007. http://
                         blogs.usatoday.com/oped/2007/10/
                         a-liberals-lame.html#more.

J. S. Vernick, D.   "Regulating Firearms Dealers in the
W. Webster, and   United States: An Analysis of State
M. T. Bulzacchelli   Law and Opportunities for Improve-
                         ment," *Journal of Law, Medicine, and
                         Ethics*, Vol. 34, p. 765, 2006.

Walter Williams   "Control Criminals Not Guns," *Capi-
                         talism Magazine*, May 21, 2008.
                         www.capmag.com/
                         article.asp?ID=5185.

Index